DATE DUE

CHOOSING TRUMAN

CHOOSING TRUMAN

The Democratic Convention of 1944

ROBERT H. FERRELL

University of Missouri Press
Columbia and London

Library of Congress Cataloging-in-Publication Data

Ferrell, Robert H.
   Choosing Truman : the Democratic convention of 1944 / Robert H. Ferrell.
     p.   cm.
   Includes bibliographical references and index.
   ISBN 0-8262-0948-3
   1. Presidents—United States—Election—1944. 2. Truman, Harry S.,
1884–1972. 3. United States—Politics and government—1933–1945. 4. Democratic National Convention (1944 : Chicago, Ill.) I. Title.
E812.F47 1994
973.918'092—dc20   93-40833
                                           CIP

♾️™ This paper meets the requirements of the American National
Standard for Permanence of Paper for Printed Library Materials, Z39.48, 1984.

Designer: Rhonda Miller
Typesetter: Connell-Zeko Type & Graphics
Printer and Binder: Thomson-Shore, Inc.
Typeface: New Century Schoolbook

For William P. Hannegan and Thomas J. Walker

I think it is an interesting part of history that a man with that type of mind was so important. I don't know how long he had that type of mind, maybe he always had it. . . . Of course this oblique type of mind does muddy the ability of the people to think clearly. There may be some virtue in bringing things out clearly to people.

—*former vice-president*
Henry A. Wallace, in appraisal of
President Franklin D. Roosevelt,
Wallace oral history, 1951,
3417-18

CONTENTS

PREFACE

In the way that history sometimes moves with inevitability, a dire progression of political events became dimly visible in the summer of 1944, when President Franklin D. Roosevelt decided to run again for reelection, this time for a fourth term. He wanted to run; he enjoyed the presidency and did not want to leave it. Leaders of his party could not keep him from running; he was far too powerful a party figure for that. The party needed him because the Republicans that year nominated a formidable opponent, Governor Thomas E. Dewey of New York. But FDR was deathly ill, and once he made up his mind to run he set in motion a series of events as certain as the length of a day: he would be nominated at the Chicago convention of the Democratic party, and he would win in November, but he could not possibly survive a fourth term.

All this persuaded party leaders to prepare for the succession. They undertook to get Vice-President Henry A. Wallace out of office, for they believed he would make a poor successor to Roosevelt, and replace him with a man they could trust.

Finding an acceptable candidate proved far more difficult than they had anticipated. Part of the trouble was the ambition of Wallace to continue as vice-president; he knew the nomination meant the presidency. The president's principal White House assistant, James F. Byrnes, whom both the leaders and the president disliked, sought the vice-presidency for the same reason. Byrnes had been a senator from South Carolina and associate justice of the Supreme Court and ordinarily would not have glanced at it. The other part of the trouble in finding a replacement for the president was Roosevelt himself. He was no easy person to deal with. He refused to consider the possibility that he might die. Too, the ravages of his cardiovascular disease made him almost too tired to make up his mind about what he considered a minor concern, choosing a running mate. All these confusions delayed his decision until the very last moment. Toward the end, when indecision had become dangerous because of the strivings of Wallace and Byrnes, the party leaders were beside themselves with anxiety.

How the nomination went to Senator Harry S. Truman of Missouri, a marvelously qualified man, who was not actively seeking it, is one of the great political stories of our century, and is the subject of the pages that follow.

ACKNOWLEDGMENTS

The almost unbelievable story of how Roosevelt came to choose Truman, a man whom he admitted he hardly knew, is scattered through the presidential libraries and several collections of personal papers, not to mention the testimonies of varying quality in many books and articles. For help in bringing this story together I am indebted to several institutions and more than a few people. The Franklin D. Roosevelt Library at Hyde Park, New York, contains fleeting testimonies, but as one might expect it is hardly full of information, much of which, on Roosevelt's side, resided within the presidential mind. His assistants of course were interested in the reasons for his choice, and their curiosity welled up often in letters and memoranda. For many courtesies in the Roosevelt Library, I am grateful to its director, Verne W. Newton, and his helpful staff. The Harry S. Truman Library in Independence, Missouri, contains much more information, if only because the new president found the subject of his nomination for the vice-presidency in 1944 of intense personal interest. Curiously, for several years after taking office as president Truman was none too sure how he got there; he did not know the details of the important meeting of party leaders with President Roosevelt at the White House on July 11, 1944, until former postmaster general Frank C. Walker visited him in the oval office in January 1950 and told him. Truman's fascination with history, in this instance his own, roused him, and in his characteristic way he sent out a series of inquiries attempting to learn more of how he became the nation's thirty-third president. For much help in the Truman Library, I am grateful to its director, Benedict K. Zobrist, assistant director George Curtis, librarian Elizabeth Safly, and archivists Dennis E. Bilger, John Curry, Raymond Geselbracht, Philip D. Lagerquist, and Samuel W. Rushay.

Among collections of private papers of participants in the choice of Truman the most notable, on the Roosevelt side, is that of Byrnes, who in 1944 as director of war mobilization, with an office in the east wing of the White House, was fascinated by the vice-presidential nomination. Byrnes went to the convention with the nomination indelibly in mind, and there took down testimonies for and against his chances, in shorthand—in his early adult life he had been a court reporter. His papers at the Robert Muldrow Cooper Library of Clemson University, in Clemson, South Carolina, were invaluable. Here my thanks for hospitality and helpfulness to the library's head of special collections, Michael F. Kohl.

My heartfelt thanks to Arthur M. Schlesinger, Jr., for permission to quote from his notes of an interview with Byrnes of April 17, 1953, which notes Byrnes afterward corrected and annotated.

Vice-President Wallace's papers at the University of Iowa are disappointingly sparse, with little but routine correspondence. His diary, selections from which were edited by John M. Blum and published as *The Price of Vision* (1973), contains a few piquant details but is in the main also disappointing. Blum published almost the entire diary for the period of the convention; the unedited diary at Iowa City adds little to his account.

Then there are the papers of Frank Walker, who was in the middle of things, and did not write much at the time but wrote a good deal a decade later when seeking to compose his memoirs. He dictated several draft narratives of what happened. Never published, they are in his papers in the archives of the University of Notre Dame, in the university's Hesburgh Library in South Bend, Indiana. For their use I am indebted to archivist Wendy Schlereth and assistant archivists Jennifer A. Webber and Matthew Steffens.

I am grateful to Thomas J. Walker for many conversations about his father.

The chairman of the Democratic National Committee in 1944, Robert E. Hannegan, did not leave many papers, very little bearing on the central activity of his career (for he wanted to be known as the man—he proposed the point on innumerable occasions—who saved the country from Henry Wallace). He managed the business mainly by telephone. His widow, Mrs. Irma Hannegan, has many recollections of the Chicago convention, at which she was present. One of her duties was to carry in her purse, and sleep on at night, a letter from President Roosevelt to her husband endorsing Truman for the vice-presidency; her husband released the letter to reporters on the evening before Truman's nomination. The son of Bob and Irma Hannegan, William P. Hannegan, has also contributed much to my understanding of how the national chairman handled a matter of greatest political delicacy. Without the help of Bill Hannegan this book could not have been written.

Lois G. Hendrickson, assistant archivist of the University of Minnesota in Minneapolis, made available the papers and diary of Max Lowenthal.

Lastly the friends who offered documents, interpretations, and suggestions on the intriguing subject of the choice of Harry S. Truman: J. Garry Clifford, James W. Goodrich, Robert Guth, Charles V. Reynolds, Jr., Stephen L. Vaughn, Francis Wyman, Robert H. Zieger.

John Milton Cooper, Francis H. Heller, and John K. Hulston read and commented on the entire manuscript.

Tim Fox, editor at the University of Missouri Press, weighed every word, for which I am most grateful. My thanks also to Polly Law, editor; Jane Lago, managing editor; and Beverly Jarrett, director and editor-in-chief.

Once again the help of Lila and Carolyn.

CHOOSING TRUMAN

— 1 —

DAYS OF UNCERTAINTY

The nomination of Senator Harry S. Truman of Missouri for the vice-presidency in the summer of 1944 was tantamount to election as successor to President Franklin D. Roosevelt. It was a devious, furtive, roundabout business: at the outset, nothing was clear, and even after a White House summit meeting of leaders of the Democratic party, in which the president opted for Truman, the nomination remained uncertain.

The president was going to run again, for a fourth term; that was a certainty. He enjoyed the office, for its convenience and ceremonial, of course, but also for its power—he enjoyed wielding the power. As the years passed after his first inaugural in 1933 he came to believe that he was necessary for the country, that he was irreplaceable, that no other individual in the United States could manage affairs, foreign and domestic, with the verve, the high ability, he could muster for the task.

And as Roosevelt himself desired the presidency, so did the party leaders want him to run again in 1944. That year the Republicans were running the former "buster" of rackets in New York City, Thomas E. Dewey, a young man of forty-two, by then governor of New York, an office in which he had been as successful as that of district attorney. Dewey was a formidable candidate. His youth bespoke activity that the tired Roosevelt could not imitate, even in appearance; in reality, to be sure, the president was tired indeed. Dewey could claim to be a new broom after eleven years of the Democracy, wherein the party of Roosevelt had worn itself out in meeting the challenges of the Great Depression and, now, World War II. Against those claims, in which there was more than a grain of truth, only "the champ," the Democrats' greatest vote-getter since President Andrew Jackson a century and more before, could have assured victory. No other Democrat could have stood against Dewey and won.

The physical problem remained. The leaders were not sure what was ailing Roosevelt, why he seemed to have more bronchitis than usual, why after the Teheran Conference of November–December 1943 he came home ill and had not bounced back. He was obviously tired, and the tiredness was showing around his eyes, the dark circles widening. He had suffered a stomach upset at Teheran. Early in 1944 during a stay at the South Carolina estate of the financier Bernard M. Baruch, he had two more such attacks. His weight was dropping. There was talk of cancer. The party leaders were no medical men and were guessing, and for the most part guessing wrongly, because what ailed the president was far-advanced cardiovascular disease. His systolic pressure was up to alarming proportions, the diastolic up too. On March 27, 1944, he underwent a general physical examination at Bethesda Naval Hospital and was seen by the staff cardiologist, Lieutenant Commander Howard G. Bruenn, who found him in heart failure. His personal physician, Vice-Admiral Ross T. McIntire, surgeon general of the U.S. Navy, an ear, nose, and throat man, had been misdiagnosing him. Bruenn put him on digitalis, which helped his heart, making it more efficient. He could do little for the pressure (this was before the era of blood-pressure pills) other than place the president on a diet. At 180 pounds he was overweight, all his weight being in his arms and chest, his legs and hips having atrophied. From the wrong evidence—the tiredness and stomach upsets and weight loss—the leaders came to the right conclusion: Roosevelt could not survive the rigors of a fourth term that would include ending the war and taking the nation through the toils of reconversion to peacetime pursuits.[1]

One would have thought it possible to explain all this to Roosevelt and get him to pay attention to whomever he chose as his running mate. That, however, was not possible. He was such a difficult mixture of traits. Immensely intelligent, his mind was a gigantic trap for any unwary visitor to the oval office; he could catch all the nuances of conversation. And he was hypersensitive to criticism of any sort. As Truman would remark after the president had passed on, he was an enormous egotist.[2] Moreover, he was manipulative; he enjoyed pushing people around. He also delighted in keeping people unsure of his intentions. Perhaps his daughter, Anna, who knew him well, certainly better than her mother, from whom he had been estranged for many years, put these latter two qualities best in a description to a friend of Vice-President Henry A. Wallace: "He is cold, calculating and shrewd and you can't tell what he will do."[3] He was not planning for any collapse of his health. He never gave any thought to the possibility of death. "No, I don't think he had the slightest idea that he was going downhill in the way he was," his daughter told an interviewer years later.[4] He believed he would continue in the White House for not merely a fourth term but a fifth, maybe more.

It was impossible to get through to the president, to tell him exactly what was at issue. This reduced everything to indirection. It opened the way to a dangerous—the presidency itself was at stake—uncertainty.

1

As best they could, the leaders of the Democratic party sought to prepare for a presidential succession, which meant placing a reliable person in the vice-presidency. They knew they did not want Vice-President Wallace, for they believed him an unfit successor to the president, and they engaged in a virtual conspiracy to get him out of the running. The White House meeting of July 11, in which they and the president chose Truman, was the culmination of this movement. The plan had begun when the secretary and acting treasurer of the Democratic National Committee, a California oilman named Edwin W. Pauley, got together with the president's appointments secretary, Major General Edwin M. (Pa) Watson, to bring in people who would speak ill of Wallace to the president, and keep out of the oval office those individuals who might be Wallace supporters. As Pauley remembered what happened, "It was during one of my visits to the White House I had a huddle with Pa. We decided then that he should arrange appointments with Roosevelt for all potential convention delegates whom we knew were opposed to Wallace. That way, the word would really get to the President."[5] To this end the conspirators enlisted the party's national chairman, Robert E. Hannegan, an erstwhile city chairman from St. Louis to whom Truman was greatly beholden for eight thousand machine votes during his close primary race in 1940 (he carried the state by less than eight thousand votes). Hannegan brought in the postmaster general, Frank C. Walker, his predecessor as national chairman, a longtime Roosevelt partisan, and co-owner of a theater chain headquartered in Scranton and New York City.

All the while Pauley personally sought to influence the president. He saw Roosevelt frequently, and sought to ingratiate himself. Pauley was an attractive individual, a mover and shaker if ever there was one. Tall, muscular, physically impressive, as calculating and shrewd as the president but without the coldness and secretiveness, he was accustomed to figuring the odds, whether in the oil business or anything else; his modus operandi was to decide how to proceed, and move in a beeline. He usually talked politics in the blue oval room in the White House itself, right next to FDR's bedroom, a part of the house that, Pauley wrote, was the president's private province where he seemed always happiest. Often he saw him in bed, where the president liked to lounge in mornings and receive his personal physician, Admiral McIntire, together with staff members and sometimes important visitors.[6]

The Pauley-Roosevelt talks divided almost equally between politics and what the oilman described as "our few common bonds," which Pauley did his best to emphasize. He had been in a bad plane crash in 1928 and at that time seemed relegated permanently to a wheelchair. So many bones were broken that the doctors believed he was going to be paralyzed. His third, fourth, and fifth vertebrae were fused for the rest of his life. He was in a hospital for four months and wore a Thomas collar on his broken neck for a year. Earning $250 a month when injured, he came out of the hospital owing $11,000. "The president, proud of the way he had overcome his own tremendous handicap, liked to talk to me as one who knew how the world looks from a wheel chair." Pauley also had won a Class A yacht race from San Francisco to Honolulu in 1939, and that too attracted Roosevelt.

During such talks he and Roosevelt edged their way around the coming decision over the vice-presidency, and several names came up. Prominent among them was the former senator from South Carolina and former associate justice of the Supreme Court, James F.

Byrnes, who was Roosevelt's "assistant president" (as Roosevelt described him) in the White House. At the president's request Walker took Byrnes home one night, and while passing through Rock Creek Park asked him point-blank if he would be interested in becoming vice-president. As Walker remembered the answer, "Barkis indeed was willing."[7]

Another possibility was William O. Douglas, associate justice of the Supreme Court. Roosevelt told Hannegan that Douglas was a wonderful fellow. Like one of the president's other court appointees, Felix Frankfurter, Douglas never let court business preoccupy him, and he took a large interest in politics, even though he was not, strictly speaking, a party man.[8] In his mid-forties, husky, athletic, he was a great outdoorsman, and he enjoyed hiking and mountain climbing in the West, especially the Pacific Northwest. He also was an inveterate gossip and teller of off-color stories, both of which must have appealed to the president.

Senator Alben W. Barkley of Kentucky, the party's majority leader, was interested in the vice-presidency. Barkley had been eyeing it for years, wishing he could have it, and the more so in 1943–1944 when Roosevelt's health turned down and the office began to mean much more than just the vice-presidency. A paunchy orator from Paducah, who needed a half hour to get started, he appeared to be only a remote possibility. Behind his senatorial bonhomie he was acutely intelligent and would have been a good choice.

There was talk of the Pacific coast shipbuilder Henry J. Kaiser, who had a reputation for being a whirlwind-like character, just the man for the vice-presidency, until the president's speechwriter, Judge Samuel I. Rosenman, known officially as his "special counsel," turned up the fact that Kaiser had made a speech in favor of a sales tax.[9]

Pauley favored Sam Rayburn of Texas, Speaker of the House of Representatives. Pauley and the Democratic leader of the Bronx, Edward J. Flynn, a longtime Roosevelt associate, a tall and handsome man who enjoyed classical music and whose tastes paralleled those of the president, arranged to have lunch with Rayburn and explained their problem with Wallace and the president. Rayburn instantly understood it. He liked the idea of becoming president, but thought the possibility of the vice-presidential nomination remote, for too many people were in the field. He told them to go ahead, if they thought it would do some good.[10]

Then there was the possibility of Truman. Like Rayburn, he too was attractive. Pauley scheduled the two of them for a series of what he described as George Washington dinners, banquets for influential groups of people followed by intimate talk, at which one or the other spoke on patriotic themes. He reported that they made good speakers, enthused audiences, and helped bring in money for the forthcoming campaign. The party treasurer received a number of complaints from supporters of Vice-President Wallace, asking why Wallace could not be scheduled as a dinner speaker. The Californian found one excuse or another not to schedule him, and afterward remarked that he was divisive, tended to make people absent themselves from audiences. More to the point was the fact that Pauley did not like him and much admired party professionals like Truman and Rayburn.

As the weeks and months passed prior to the convention, Rayburn's star began to fall, through no fault of his own. In Texas there was much anti-Roosevelt sentiment, and the conservative Democrats rallied around a slate of delegates for the convention that won out against Rayburn and his friends. The Texas Supreme Court certified the slate as the state's legal delegation, against a group of disappointed opponents who promised to take the fight to the credentials committee at the convention. This meant a public fight over Texas's votes. More to the point, it meant that Rayburn could not control his own state. The dissidents indeed turned against him personally and sought to take his House seat, putting up $250,000 of oil money against him; as he described matters he had the "fight of his life." The primary in Texas was on the fourth Saturday in July, and he was so hard-pressed he could not even attend the convention. All this meant that nationally speaking he was in an impossible position. By the time the convention approached, his candidacy for the vice-presidency had much diminished.[11]

Where did this put Truman among the candidates? There was, of course, much to recommend him. The Missouri senator came from a border state, meaning he was in the South but not of it; he could get the support of southern delegates at the convention without having associated with southern causes, especially the principal cause, the denial of civil rights to black Americans. Moreover, by 1944 he had spent nearly ten years in the Senate, and he had handled well his wartime committee to investigate the national defense program. The Truman Committee, as it was known, avoided criticism of the president, unlike the Civil War committee that bedeviled President Abraham Lincoln. Roosevelt actually acquired the notion, presumably from thinking about it, that he himself had organized the Truman Committee. In actual fact he had nothing to do with it; a newspaperman from Kansas City, William P. Helm, suggested the idea early in 1941, and Truman seized upon it. The committee's work had not been helped by the initial parsimony of Senator Byrnes, who would be one of Truman's two principal rivals at the 1944 convention. One of Byrnes's duties in the Senate was to allot money to committees, and he allotted fifteen thousand dollars to investigate the expenditure of tens of billions. Roosevelt's hand might have been in that parsimony—what better way to kill a committee than give it no money? But when the committee became a great success the president took credit, rubbing his chin reflectively and saying to visitors, "Yes . . . yes. . . . I put him in charge of that war investigating committee, didn't I?"[12]

Too, Truman as vice-president could help with the peace treaties and the United Nations Charter when those instruments came before the Senate, unlike Vice-President Wallace, who as the Senate's presiding officer had managed to antagonize nearly every member of the Upper House by paying no attention to senators, singly or collectively.[13] Aloof, even ethereal, Wallace spent much of his time on trips abroad, visiting foreign nations and peoples, representing the president.

Truman's earlier connection with the Thomas J. Pendergast political machine in Kansas City would not have bothered Roosevelt, for Truman had done nothing improper as a result of the association. The president sometimes pointed out to Rosenman that he, FDR, had graduated from the Tammany Hall district club led by James J. (Jimmy) Hines, who, like Pendergast, went to jail.[14]

The trouble was that Roosevelt did not know the Missouri senator well. Speaking privately in the weeks before the convention he admitted, "I hardly know Truman. He has been over here a few times, but he made no particular impression on me." The later president

liked to remember that during his wartime years in the Senate he
saw Roosevelt a great deal, off the record. As chairman of the special
investigating committee he was an important figure and afterward
wrote, "I had been in the habit of seeing the President at least once a
week, and more often if he thought it necessary, about matters that
came before the committee." In 1952 he told an Indiana high-school
principal that after the election of 1944 he saw him nearly every day.
In a taped interview in 1959 he related, "I used to get in the back
door once or twice a week. Nobody knew that." But Jonathan Daniels, a wartime White House staff member, later a Truman biographer, thought all this a great exaggeration. In remarks to newspaper
reporters in 1944, Truman unwittingly agreed. At the convention
the senator told reporters he had neither seen nor spoken with Roosevelt since March 5.[15]

Two events early in 1944 seemed later to show that the decision
would go to Truman, but one may never have happened and the
other was not at all conclusive. The leaders may have had a meeting
with the president in January 1944 at the White House. So wrote
George E. Allen, who by this time had taken over the party's secre-
taryship from Pauley, who remained as treasurer. A roly-poly, quick-
witted Washington man-about-the-city, collector of corporation di-
rectorships and later friend of presidents Truman and Eisenhower
(and author of the gossipy book, *Presidents Who Have Known Me*),
Allen claimed a meeting, although he admitted he was not there.
According to him the meeting looked to the nomination of Truman.[16]

That same month Hannegan was chosen chairman of the national
committee, and presumably the appearance in this crucial post of a
man who was a Truman protégé marked a major rise in Truman's
fortunes. The ebullient Hannegan was in his early forties and full of
energy, just the individual to promote a fellow Missourian. Son of a
St. Louis chief of detectives, a four-letter man at St. Louis University, and later a professional football and baseball player, he went to
law school and easily moved into politics. The husky, strapping,
smiling Hannegan, at the age of twenty-nine, took over management
of the Twenty-first Ward in his native city, a ward that had not gone
Democratic in living memory. It voted Democratic three months later.
He allied with Mayor Bernard F. Dickmann, he and the mayor creating
what was known to the *St. Louis Post-Dispatch* as the Hannegan-

Dickmann machine. In the Senate primary of 1940, in which Truman fought for his political life against Governor Lloyd C. Stark and the Pendergast prosecutor, District Attorney Maurice Milligan, Hannegan saved the day by marshaling enough votes to get Truman renominated.

Senator Truman had become Hannegan's mentor when the Hannegan-Dickmann machine fell apart during an internal party squabble in 1941. Truman initially acquired for Hannegan the district collectorship of internal revenue, announcing to reporters, "Hannegan carried St. Louis three times for the President and for me. If he is not nominated there will be no Collector at St. Louis." The collectorship had been a sinkhole, the worst in the country, and with Hannegan's appointment the *Post-Dispatch* announced the end of the world, devoting a full page to the subject of "ex-Boss Hannegan" about to get a $6,500 a year job. To the newspaper's surprise Hannegan cleaned up the office, so much so that next year the Roosevelt administration brought him to Washington as commissioner. Early in 1944, Postmaster General Walker, who doubled as national chairman, found his dual duties too much and asked to give up the chairmanship. He first made an overture to Truman. According to Walker (contrary to Truman) he did not offer the senator the job. In any event Truman, busy with his committee, did not want it. Truman recommended Hannegan.[17]

Truman instructed Hannegan how to accept the national chairmanship. He told him, a wise appraisal, not to take the job unless the president asked him. Neither Truman nor Hannegan expected the president to call, but he did. Hannegan phoned Truman and inquired, "What do I do now, coach?" The senator laughed and said, "You take it."[18]

Actually Hannegan was a natural choice for the appointment. It later was said that Truman put Hannegan in the party chairmanship to work for him. The circumstances of Hannegan's appointment testify against the theory. It was none too sure who his sponsor was. It might even have been Byrnes, who recommended him to the president, who in turn responded in two sentences, dated January 10, saying Hannegan was fine.[19] Consider also the time when the appointment occurred—in January 1944—which was before the vice-presidential issue had become serious. Truman was not yet sensitive to the possibility that he would become a candidate. If he had been, he might have maneuvered to take the national chairmanship himself. He never would have advised Hannegan to let the president ask for him, for the president, a proud man, might well not have done so.[20]

The truth is that Truman's situation even in the spring of 1944 was altogether unclear, although his name had risen and Pauley favored him or Rayburn, and Hannegan was his protégé. The anti-Wallace movement was going along splendidly; it was far advanced, and the Pauley conspiracy with Pa Watson had brought in enough hostile testimonies that the president was turning against Wallace, beyond question. Everyone (save the president, who did not know about it) agreed with Pauley's remark to oval office visitors: "You are not nominating a Vice President of the United States, but a President." Still, Roosevelt could choose any running mate he wanted. The party needed him against Governor Dewey. The party leaders were not powerful enough to dictate a running mate.

It is possible that Hannegan did manage, as he later claimed, to convince Roosevelt about Truman, but it seems unlikely. In any event the story came from Hannegan himself in later years and involved his friend, Postmaster General Walker, who never said anything about it. As Hannegan remembered, matters with Roosevelt came down to a choice of Truman or Douglas. After several weeks he managed to talk the president out of "Bill" Douglas; the chairman said Douglas was not enough of a party man to have a following and hence would not be acceptable to the leaders and their followers. When he broached the subject of Truman the president suddenly turned to him, knowing what Bob Hannegan wanted to "sell," and said, "All right, Bob—start talking." Some weeks before the convention, according to Hannegan, Roosevelt virtually decided on Truman as his running mate. But this decision was known only to Hannegan and Walker.[21]

David McCullough, in his recent biography of Truman, has written that the Bronx leader, Flynn, who had known Roosevelt since the Albany days, was the man who really pushed the Missouri senator with the president and thereby made possible his nomination. Unfortunately, as with Hannegan's memories of having talked Roosevelt into accepting Truman, there is no support for any such activity by Flynn other than what he wrote in his memoirs, *You're the Boss,* published in 1947. Flynn said therein that Truman "dropped into the slot," which was true enough, in terms of Truman's qualifications. But there is no evidence that Flynn dropped him into the slot.[22]

One turns to the White House meeting of the leaders with Roosevelt, following a dinner, July 11, 1944, a bare eight days before the convention was due to open. According to Flynn, the president asked him to get a group together and, so Flynn remembered, "inject Truman into the picture."[23]

On the day of this summit conference the leaders were busy as bees, and Walker's telephone log shows that several of the dinner guests got together for lunch at the Mayflower Hotel and presumably rehearsed what they would say. Walker apparently was in charge of the rehearsal. A quiet, almost laconic, inconspicuous man (the latter trait undoubtedly endeared him to Roosevelt), balding, with a slightly mischievous twinkle in his eyes, he must have found the task amusing, as he and the other invitees sat around guessing what might be on the presidential mind.[24] The president had invited, in addition to Walker, and Flynn, who was the dinner's organizer, Hannegan, Allen, Pauley, and Mayor Edward J. Kelly of Chicago. In charge of convention arrangements, Pauley was flying in from Chicago, and did not have a chance to converse at the Mayflower. Kelly possibly was there. An old-time politico who controlled his city like a satrap, he perhaps was invited to the summit conference partly because he was to be host at the convention, partly because unlike the other leaders he could speak for the Middle West, and partly also because he was a party regular and simpatico with the others. Bulky, nondescript, he looked like a college professor, until he opened his mouth to speak in Chicago brogue; he always got to the point somehow, if not with the best choice of words.

This was the situation when the leaders on the evening of July 11 came to dine with the president. Before dinner Roosevelt mixed the martinis and the group carefully complimented him on their excellence. Pauley remembered the president was "very proud of the way he shook up his own martinis and he always waited to be assured they were the best in the world. He had that pride in everything he did well and if someone deprived him of his pleasure in making them a drink, there was always for a moment at least, a little coolness."[25]

During dinner the president noticed a strange second butler, and every time the group started talking this man seemed to be hovering around. This led him, after the butler was gone, into discussing whether he could really trust the presidential help, and he began talking of food poisoning and various attempts on his life. After dinner the company adjourned to the blue oval room and began their discussion.

The group quickly eliminated two possibilities, Rayburn and Barkley. The problem with Rayburn was that he could not get the support of his own state delegation. They all admired Barkley, and even the president seemed at ease with him, in spite of the fact that he recently had defied Roosevelt in a startling scene in the Senate. Barkley had sponsored an administration tax bill, and the assumption was that Roosevelt would sign it. When the bill passed and went up for signature the president vetoed it and announced, in a phrase that apparently was his own, that the bill would bring "relief not for the needy but for the greedy." In a fury Barkley resigned as majority leader and advised his colleagues to override. Roosevelt quickly soothed the senator and backed down, and even asked Barkley to nominate him at the convention. Because of this fracas it would have been natural for him to refuse Barkley as a running mate. Instead, at the leaders' meeting the presidential objection, and that of the others, was to Barkley's age, which was sixty-seven.

A good deal of time was spent discussing Byrnes, the president's assistant, but for two reasons he seemed unavailable. His name had come up in 1940, before the choice of Wallace, and at that time the president vetoed him because Byrnes had been born a Roman Catholic but left the church upon marriage, going over to his wife's Episcopalian faith. Roosevelt then professed to be concerned over the reaction of the millions of Irish Catholics, mostly in Eastern cities, who would have found Byrnes's apostasy unacceptable. At the meeting the president said the Catholic issue would not be so important; indeed, he considered it of little importance. What did bother him was what he was hearing from Mayor Kelly and from Flynn, that Byrnes's southern origins and views would antagonize hundreds of thousands of Negroes—Flynn guessed two or three hundred thousand in New York City alone—who would not vote for him as a result. Moreover, there was Byrnes's action in 1943, when he heard demands of American labor that because of increases in the cost of living, caused by the raising of prices by manufacturers and of rents due to the wartime housing shortage, laboring men and women needed increases in pay. With a flourish Byrnes announced a policy of "hold the line." The latter two issues, involving the Negro vote and the labor vote, removed Byrnes's name from consideration.

To the amazement of Pauley, Roosevelt raised the name of John G. Winant, ambassador to London and a former governor of New Hampshire. Winant was a big, hulking man, who according to the president could make the "rottenest" speech and yet when finished give the impression he was Abraham Lincoln. Why he named him is impossible to say, and his name went down as fast as it went up.

More serious, and equally amazing, was the president's discussion of Douglas. Doubtless Hannegan and Walker thought they had gotten Douglas out of sight, but he popped up again. Mayor Kelly may have brought him up; Kelly, Walker remembered, had read a magazine article about Douglas, the writer of which had gotten in touch with Kelly, who in turn became enthusiastic about Douglas. But the president himself waxed lyrical about Douglas's attractions. He said he had the following of the left wing of the American people, the same following Wallace had; that he had experience from the backwoods of the Northwest as a logger; and that "he looked and acted on occasions like a Boy Scout, and would have, in his opinion, appeal at the polls—and, besides, played an interesting game of poker."[26]

When Roosevelt finished talking about Douglas there was dead silence on the part of everyone, for no one wanted Douglas—he was not as offbeat as Wallace but possessed the same amateur political status. The president easily sensed this.

There was quite a bit of discussion about Truman. As Walker remembered, Hannegan did not really advance Truman's candidacy. "I do not think that is true. In all my discussions with Hannegan not once did he advocate the candidacy of Truman merely because of their friendship. I think he weighed Truman in the balance, just as everybody else did."[27] Roosevelt inquired about Truman's age, and the president's son-in-law, the newspaperman John Boettiger, husband of Anna Roosevelt, who was acting as a presidential aide and joined the meeting after dinner, volunteered to go out and find a congressional directory and see how old Truman was. When he returned with the book, Pauley took it and hid it in his lap, for by that time the conversation had turned elsewhere. Everyone other than the president knew Truman was born in 1884, two years after Roosevelt.

The conversation began to wear itself out, and finally the president turned to Hannegan and said, "Bob, I think you and everyone else want Truman!" Exactly what Roosevelt said varied with the auditor, but Pauley thought that before Hannegan could reply the president put his hand on his knee and said, "If that's the case, it's Truman."[28] The meeting broke up, after an assignment of tasks by the president. He told Walker to see Byrnes and tell him he was out; he felt he had a "half commitment" to Byrnes. Hannegan was to see Wallace. Pauley was to call Rayburn, then in Bonham, Texas.[29] The secretary of the Senate, Les Biffle, not present, was to call Barkley.

When the group was downstairs waiting to get in their cars, Walker told Hannegan to use a pretext, such as that he had left his jacket (the evening had been warm and Roosevelt insisted that his guests take off their jackets), and go back upstairs and have the president put his decision in writing. Hannegan went up, and while he was there Pauley came into the room looking for his own jacket, which it turned out Hannegan had taken, only to hear Roosevelt saying to Hannegan, "I know this makes you boys happy, and you are the ones I am counting on to win this election. But I still think Douglas would have the greater public appeal."[30] Both assured him that what Truman might lack in appeal they would make up in enthusiasm. The president gave the chairman a note on a piece of scratch paper. When Hannegan came downstairs he patted his coat pocket and said to Walker, "I've got it."[31]

2

It was one thing for the leaders and president to hold a meeting and arrive at a decision, but something else to ensure that what came out of the meeting would prevail. Three factors were going to affect the decision of Tuesday evening. One was the intense desire of both Wallace and Byrnes to gain the vice-presidential nomination, for which they were willing to push very hard indeed. Both wanted the nomination more than anything else they had sought in their political careers, for they knew it meant the presidency, which they knew they could not hope to get on their own; each man could only come into it by what one might describe as inheritance. Wallace was an avowed liberal, whose supporters were ardent New Dealers. This might have seemed no disqualification, save that beginning in 1937 with Roosevelt's effort to enlarge the Supreme Court the country began to turn conservative. The idea of liberalism still carried immense appeal, and if one asked the man or woman in the street if he or she were a New Dealer the answer would have been yes. But liberalism as an ideology was losing its attraction, and by 1944 the good economic times of the war era made it seem almost unnecessary. Too, Wallace's supporters, labor unions and the small fringe of American radicals—socialists and a few communists—affronted the more moderate liberals, if one might so describe them; they did not like the militancy of wartime union leaders, nor the socialist-communists. Wallace's own lack of personal charm, his statements to reporters that he preferred to deal with issues rather than people, did not help his cause. On Byrnes's side the principal problem in running for the presidency was not that he had been born into the Catholic church, as Roosevelt had said, but that he was from the South and carried the burden of his section's racial attitudes.

The second factor that made uncertain the decision of the summit conference was the president's very special method of dealing with people. Ordinarily it worked, but sometimes it was exceedingly slow, and in dealing with determined people it just might not work. Eleanor Roosevelt once told Jonathan Daniels, "He always hopes to get things settled pleasantly and he won't realize that there are times when you have to do an unpleasant thing directly and perhaps unpleasantly."[32] But she was none too acute in understanding her husband, and the president's way was a bit more complicated. In politics, which Roosevelt considered a marvelously intricate game, the best result when decisions came was to avoid having anyone become angry with him. Unpleasantness, he well knew, sometimes was necessary, and his arrangement was to have subordinates inflict it. At the end of the Tuesday evening leaders' conference when the president assigned Walker to see Byrnes, Walker gently protested the assignment, and Roosevelt brought him up short. He told the postmaster general in so many words, and Walker remembered it a decade later, that this was the way the game was played.[33]

The third factor, which imperceptibly could ally itself with the second, was the president's poor health. It was possible that he could become so tired he would give in to a candidate who pushed hard enough.

Wallace's case came up first. The vice-president was a tall, athletic man who often arose in mornings and played tennis. He belied his fifty-three years, looking like a much younger man, perhaps a college youth, what with his tousled hair and zealous, intense face. He came from a family of farm journalists, of which he was the third generation. His grandfather, Henry Wallace, had been editor of *Wallaces' Farmer,* a journal that circulated throughout the Middle West and told farmers how to plant and market crops. His father, Henry C. Wallace, became secretary of agriculture in the cabinet of Harding, and stayed into the Coolidge era, dying in 1924. Meanwhile the later vice-president took over the editorship of the family journal. During the 1920s, Henry Agard Wallace made a name for himself among farmers by breeding corn, and his Pioneer Hi-Bred Corn Company made him wealthy. He was an early supporter of Roosevelt, and the president in 1933 named him secretary of agriculture, which post he held until 1941 when he became vice-president.

All this was to Wallace's credit, but there admittedly were deficit items. The vice-president possessed a mystical bent, which did not do him any good politically. As Pauley described him, with more than a touch of sarcasm, "He was so much the prophet, an unworldly man of mystical leanings and ideas, that it was obvious to all who knew him that he would only make the country a mighty strange president." Wallace had been interested in the ideas of the Russian mystic Nicholas Roerich, and had corresponded extensively with Frances R. Grant, the vice-president of the Roerich Museum in New York. The then secretary of agriculture had referred to Roerich as the "Guru"; he reported seeing visions of the Guru in his morning meditations, which renewed his strength. The letters contained coded references and some disparaging remarks about Wallace's associates. He described Secretary of State Cordell Hull as the Sour One, and Roosevelt as the Flaming One or the Wavering One, depending on whether or not he approved the president's actions. He told his correspondent that FDR was "undoubtedly an agent through which great forces are working, but he is as provoking to me in the density

of his perceptions at times as I doubtless am to you." He described
the Soviet Union as a tiger, and he said he had sent "an effective
tiger letter" to Hull and Roosevelt. He spoke allegorically of the
Dark Ones, the Steadfast Ones, and "dugpas," and beseeched the
blessings of the Great Ones. All of which led him into a most embarrassing fix: the letters passed into the hands of the Pittsburgh newspaper publisher Paul Block, who sent them to the Democratic national convention in Chicago in 1940, perhaps to amuse the delegates.
According to Roosevelt's press secretary, Stephen T. Early, who years
later regaled the diners at the White House lunchroom with the
story, heroic measures had to be taken. The party flew the New York
attorney Morris Ernst out to Chicago just ahead of Block's representative bearing the documents, and threatened dire penalties, including libel. Ernst apparently secured the correspondence, Pa Watson
locked it up in the White House safe, and presumably it still was
there in the summer of 1944.[34]

Another problem was that as presiding officer of the Senate, Wallace was not at all a success. His mind was not in it; he paid no
attention to the senators. Upon himself becoming vice-president,
Truman early in 1945 remarked pointedly to a newspaperman, "In
the past four years I doubt if there are half a dozen Senators all told
who have been in the Vice President's office. You can draw your own
conclusions."[35] Wallace simply was uninterested. The majority leader,
Barkley, "advised Henry in a friendly way" to give more attention to
his work, and Wallace gave no attention. According to Barkley, "he
always took my suggestions in good spirit and thanked me for them,
but it never seemed to make any impression."[36] Wallace preferred
international missions.

Russia fascinated the vice-president, and he took lessons in the
Russian language. This led to an episode that completely "turned
off" Pauley when he heard of it. Early in the war Wallace was taking
Russian lessons from Colonel C. M. Paul, and at midnight after a
lesson he challenged the colonel, a younger and smaller man, to a
footrace from Wallace's apartment in the Wardman Park Hotel back
to Paul's room at the Mayflower Hotel. Wallace paced Paul all the
way down, and when the colonel, who was carrying books, com-
plained, with his tongue hanging out, Wallace told him that surely
he was not going to let an older man beat him. The colonel barely

made it. But Pauley wondered what might have happened if, say, some FBI man saw Paul chasing the vice-president of the United States all the way to the Mayflower.[37]

Gradually, and doubtless mainly because of Pauley's campaign, Wallace lost the president's confidence. Testimony in the oval office by individuals who would be delegates to the convention must have convinced Roosevelt he could not afford to run with a man who would lose votes for the ticket. A lesser reason for disliking Wallace was that FDR's wife was pressing him hard to accept Wallace for another term, and anything Mrs. Roosevelt wanted became automatically something the president did not want.[38]

It is difficult to be sure when the president took the first move to get Wallace out of the vice-presidency, but it seems to have been sometime early in May 1944, after Hannegan saw Roosevelt and told him of the vice-president's unsuitabilities. The president told the national chairman to talk to Wallace. Instead, as matters turned out, Wallace went to see Hannegan. "The President," he said, "told me I should talk to you." Afterward Hannegan told Byrnes what happened, saying he never had such an experience in his life—there he was, a country boy, telling the vice-president of the United States he should not be renominated. Wallace, he said, acted like a high-school boy, looking down sheepishly, raking his toe on the floor. Hannegan gave him the word—said he had been across the country several times, talked to Democratic leaders everywhere, and their only concern was to get Wallace off the ticket. The vice-president, flabbergasted, asked if Hannegan had talked to the right people, and otherwise gave no evidence of what he would do, though Hannegan believed he would tell the president he did not want to be renominated.[39]

Not long afterward, on May 20, Wallace left on a trip to Asia. The trip must have been another part of Roosevelt's plan to get him off the ticket. Because of the president's increasing doubts about Wallace's suitability for a second term, it was convenient to get him out of the country so he could not organize his supporters for the convention. The place where the president sent him, incidentally, is interesting. The vice-president had asked to go on a trip to the Soviet Union. His diary, which he was keeping assiduously, so testifies. Roosevelt doubtless encouraged him. But the western USSR was not where he went. The president had a puckish sense of humor, and that may be why he sent him to Outer Mongolia, China, and, lastly, Siberia. One suspects he included the latter locality on purpose, for he could tell visitors with a smile that he had sent "Henry" to Siberia.

Prior to the trip Roosevelt took a precaution. He thought that when the vice-president went to China he might take the "wrong people" with him—that is, people who believed China could teach democracy to the world. He had his daughter, Anna, check on passengers in the vice-president's plane.[40]

On June 2, speaking with three of his assistants including Daniels, who was keeping a diary, the president showed how his mind was moving. To the group he said, "Of course, everybody knows I am for Henry Wallace."[41] He went on to say he had thought the feeling against Wallace had been largely that of politicians but was beginning to believe it went down below. Some people had told him it meant forty percent of the vote in their localities. If one cut that in half, and half again, it still could mean loss of one or two million votes. He already had instructed Henry what to say when the vice-president returned and made a report to the American people. "Well, I told him what to say—it is going to be perfectly banal, pointing out the great trade possibilities for America in China and Siberia after the war." He was not about to have Wallace use a national radio hookup to advance his plans for the vice-presidential nomination. Then he came to the point: "I think one or two persons ought to go out and meet Wallace and tell him about this feeling about his political liability."

This conference with his assistants was quite interesting. The president explained his doubts about Wallace by resorting to history. When he had needed to replace Vice-President John N. Garner in 1940 (a conservative, Garner was no longer useful, as Roosevelt and the country were turning conservative, and Garner anyway was aspiring to the presidency), Roosevelt had first resorted to Secretary of State Cordell Hull, but "he sat in my room while I was in bed for three hours and just said he wouldn't be Vice-President." That is, Hull, like Garner, wanted the presidency. His second choice, the president said, was Jimmy Byrnes, but he talked with Archbishop Francis Spellman of New York and others in the Catholic church who said Byrnes would not do.[42] At the last minute he decided on Wallace. The burden of these details was that Wallace was a stopgap in 1940 and was hardly essential in 1944. And if the conversation had gotten back to Wallace it would have discouraged the vice-president without his chief, the president, having openly done so.

About this time the president saw the head of the Congress of Industrial Organizations, Philip Murray, who made an eloquent plea for Wallace. It obviously had been impossible for Pa Watson to keep an important figure like Murray out of the oval office. While Murray talked, Roosevelt puffed at a cigarette and looked at the ceiling. After Murray finished, FDR said, disconcertingly, "Oh, you are talking about the Yogi Man." Murray was mystified, not understanding. The president's comment hardly supported Wallace's candidacy.[43]

The president carried out his plan of having someone meet Wallace by first enlisting his special counsel, Sam Rosenman. "You remember," FDR asked him, "how in our Albany days whenever I had some unpleasant message to deliver to the political leaders or officials in New York City, I used to let you have the pleasure of bearing the bad news?" He smiled as he said it, adding, "I am going to let you have that pleasure again." He told Rosenman he wanted him to fly out to meet Wallace at Seattle—the vice-president's plane was due in Seattle on Sunday, July 9—and fly back with him. He was to tell him it was impossible to fight for him again, as in 1940, without risk of creating a permanent split in the party. Roosevelt added sweetly, "I am sure he will understand and be glad to step down."[44]

Rosenman had to accept the assignment, and immediately was in trouble; he knew Wallace would fight for the nomination. He called the vice-president's office in Washington and a veritable tangle ensued, probably on purpose, he thought. Regardless of how hard he pressed to get aboard Wallace's plane, it proved impossible.

The delay brought further confusion in the person of Secretary of the Interior Harold L. Ickes, whom the president invited into the enterprise of stopping Wallace. The three—Roosevelt, Rosenman, and Ickes—lunched on Thursday, July 7. The president needed to organize things immediately, as that evening he would be seeing Mrs. Lucy Rutherfurd, who was visiting in Washington. He was planning to dine with her the next evening, and would spend the weekend with her in Shangri-La, his secret hideaway near Thurmont, Maryland, during which he would have no appointments.[45]

Unlike Rosenman, Ickes accepted the assignment with joy. He (so Rosenman believed, and it was true) was himself receptive to the vice-presidential nomination. The president doubtless knew this and hence brought him into the Rosenman mission.

During the presidential luncheon on Thursday the secretary of the interior asked the president what he and Rosenman were to propose to Wallace in the way of public service. According to Ickes's diary, "He said that he would make him Ambassador to China where he would fit in well."[46]

By all measurements the Ickes-Rosenman mission should have been a great success. Ickes and Rosenman balanced each other off very neatly. The secretary of the interior, a bulky man with a snub nose, was a tough old Progressive: he once had been a supporter of Theodore Roosevelt. Entitling his memoirs *The Autobiography of a Curmudgeon* (1943), he could lend curmudgeonly éclat to the forthcoming proceedings with the vice-president of the United States. Too, he envisioned himself a political insider, loving political gossip and cramming his diary with it; the Wallace mission was right down his alley. Rosenman, on the other hand, small and moon-faced, retiring, the silent type, could deftly bring diplomacy to the occasion. He could be counted on to say things cautiously and tentatively but with just enough point to make the auditor certain of what he was hearing.

The Wallace plane arrived in Washington on Monday morning, July 10, at 9:30. The vice-president had been gone fifty-one days, traveling twenty-seven thousand miles. He telephoned Roosevelt at 10:00. He was told the president was bathing, and an appointment was made for late that afternoon. Rosenman thereupon had Pa Watson tell Wallace the president wanted him to see Ickes and Rosenman before Wallace's appointment at the oval office, which was at 4:30. Wallace invited the two to lunch at his apartment in the Wardman Park.

Alas, the Rosenman-Ickes mission was an utter failure. The talk perhaps turned out the way it did because Ickes did not talk enough and Rosenman talked too much and did the job in glancing fashion. Sam, according to Wallace, "created the impression that the President wanted me but he either did not think I could win in the convention nor help him win in the fall." Wallace told them haughtily he had an engagement with the president that afternoon and did not want to talk politics. According to the vice-president, "They beat a hasty retreat." On the way out Wallace, so Ickes wrote in his diary, "complimented me upon my virility." The vice-president had seen an account in a newspaper, by the gossip columnist Walter Winchell, to the effect that Ickes's young wife, Jane, was going to have another baby. (Ickes disgustedly described it as another of Winchell's "wild guesses.")[47]

The two messengers, crestfallen, went back to the White House and told Roosevelt. On the way back Ickes told Rosenman that Wallace had known full well they had authority to speak for the president and that what he, Ickes, objected to was Wallace's noble attitude. He said it gave him a pain.[48]

There followed Wallace's talk with the president that afternoon and lunches on Tuesday and Thursday. None of these meetings was satisfactory, for Roosevelt was not going to tell Wallace directly he was out and Wallace was not going to accept anything less than FDR's word.

The Monday talk showed Roosevelt being almost merciless—it was almost cruel to get his vice-president of nearly four years into the oval office, after the long trip abroad, and treat him the way the president did. Wallace opened the conversation with a two-hour commentary about his trip, and gave Roosevelt some Outer Mongolian stamps (he had been the first American official to enter Mongolia in seventeen years). After these preliminaries the president said that when Wallace went out the vice-president should say they had not discussed politics. Roosevelt then said, "I am now talking to the ceiling about political matters." He said Wallace was his choice as a running mate and he was willing to make a statement to that effect. Wallace asked if he would say, "If I were a delegate to the convention I would vote for Henry Wallace." The answer: "Yes, I would." The president added that people were advising against Wallace's nomination unless the president said what he did in 1940, that it would be himself and Wallace or neither; Wallace broke in to remark that he did not want to be pushed down anybody's throat but did need to know whether Roosevelt wanted him. The president again gave his assurance. Wallace pushed the point: "Mr. President, if you can find anyone who will add more strength to the ticket than I, by all means take him." The president did not say he agreed with people who said the vice-president would cost the ticket one to three million votes (FDR was raising the figure he had related privately to his assistants), but rather that he could not bear to see Wallace's name put up before the convention and rejected. Wallace said he had been in difficult situations before. "But you have your family to think of," explained Roosevelt. "Think of the catcalls and jeers and the definiteness of rejection." Wallace said, "I am not worried about my family." Whereupon the president asked him back for lunch on Tuesday and Thursday.[49]

That evening and the next day, Monday and Tuesday, July 10–11, a third presidential envoy, Senator Joseph P. Guffey of Pennsylvania, talked to the vice-president and tried his best to talk him out of the nomination. Guffey was a bit of a busybody, and it is possible that he designated himself as an envoy. In 1943 he had taken Truman out into the garden of his Washington house and asked what the Missouri senator thought of Wallace's record as vice-president. Truman said Wallace was the best secretary of agriculture the country ever had. Guffey, laughing, said that was what he thought. He then asked Truman if he, Truman, would be a candidate for the vice-presidency; Truman said he would not. At the Chicago convention (to move the story ahead a bit) Guffey would forget all this and become a great Wallace supporter, cheering Wallace onward toward another four years in the vice-presidential office. Whatever, Joe Guffey on Monday and Tuesday was working for Roosevelt and duly reported Wallace's position back to headquarters. He spoke with Wallace for an hour on Monday night, in the presence of two Wallace intimates, and in the words of whoever in Roosevelt's office reported the conversation to the president, "All three of them seem to think, in spite of what Joe said, that Wallace could be nominated at the Convention." According to Guffey, Wallace was quite stubborn about it. On Tuesday, shortly after noon, Guffey called Wallace's apartment, and a Wallace assistant read off the kind of statement the vice-president wanted from the president, which was "out of the question," something about "we have made a team which pulls together, thinks alike and plans alike." Joe recommended that the president make clear to Wallace that "Wallace is his first choice and that he would vote for Wallace at the Convention if he were a delegate, but that the Convention will have to decide." He was going to see the vice-president again that afternoon, alone, and promised to report back.[50]

The vice-president's Tuesday lunch with the president took place just after Guffey called. At the lunch Wallace gave Roosevelt a list of state delegations and estimated he had at least 290 delegates. The president whistled in surprise. Wallace said a forthcoming Gallup poll would reveal he had support of sixty-five percent of Democratic voters, compared to seventeen for Barkley, five for Rayburn, three for Byrnes, two for Douglas, and two for Truman. "Well, I'll be damned!" said Roosevelt. The president moved in on Wallace again, in his typically tangential way, and Wallace again engaged in fancy footwork. Roosevelt said many people looked on the vice-president as a communist or worse. Some referred to him with ridicule, as "that fellow" who wanted to give a quart of milk to every Hottentot. Wallace responded that he never said every Hottentot needed a quart of milk. "You know, Mr. President, I never said that. That was said for me by the President of the National Association of Manufacturers." The president professed great surprise at this news.[51]

The leaders' conference that evening eliminated Wallace and saw assignment of Hannegan to tell Wallace as much. On Wednesday morning around noontime Hannegan performed his mission. He did not use kid gloves with the vice-president, as Ickes and Rosenman had done on Monday and Guffey perhaps had done that evening and the next day. In Wallace's words, put in his diary some days later, "He said he wanted to tell me that I did not have a chance. He said I ought to withdraw." By Wednesday morning, however, Wallace knew what to expect and refused to deal with the chairman of the national committee, virtually insulting him. He told one of his lieutenants what he was going to say, and the lieutenant even told a reporter for the *Post-Dispatch,* Edwin A. Harris, to go over to the Wardman Park where, the lieutenant said, when he arrived he would see Hannegan emerging red-faced from the vice-president's apartment. Hannegan emerged red-faced.[52]

The lunch conversation on Thursday was only a repetition of the discouragements of Monday, Tuesday, and Wednesday. It did show a considerable ingenuity on Roosevelt's part, again to no avail. Roosevelt told him about the meeting with the Democratic chieftains. "According to the President they all thought I would harm the ticket. I said at once to the President, 'If you think so, I will withdraw at once.' . . . He said it was mighty sweet of me to make the offer but he could not think of accepting it." As Wallace remembered, when he was preparing to leave the president "drew me close and turned on his full smile and a very hearty handclasp," and said, "While I cannot put it just that way in public, I hope it will be the same old team." As he was nearing the door the president ended with, "Even though they do beat you out at Chicago, we will have a job for you in world economic affairs."[53]

Wallace thus failed to withdraw. He pretended to be obtuse, taking Roosevelt's words at face value when he knew full well what they meant. There was no doubt in his mind, he later wrote, as to the president's intentions after the return from the Far East: "He wanted to ditch me as noiselessly as possible." The vice-president professed to believe Roosevelt changed momentarily when his, Wallace's, presentation "clearly indicated that he had been lied to by his advisers."[54]

To make the situation worse, failing to get things straight with the vice-president after the leaders' meeting declared him out and Truman in, the president gave him the promised letter of endorsement. It was a most unfortunate thing to do but so typical of Roosevelt. The endorsement took the form of a letter to a Wallace supporter, Senator Samuel D. Jackson of Indiana, who was to be permanent chairman of the convention, and turned out to be as ambiguous as the face-to-face presidential conversations. Dated Friday, July 14, when the president planned to be at Hyde Park, it was drafted the day after the leaders' meeting, July 12, and went through at least two revisions in Roosevelt's hand.[55] The first draft was fairly long and related what he told Wallace he would say, which was that if he himself were to be a delegate to the convention he would vote for Wallace. After this pleasantry—for he was not going to be a delegate—he placed three short paragraphs relating that he did not want to dictate to the convention, that delegates would wish to size up all candidates and make their own choice. In redrafting he made a slight change in the letter's introductory sentence; removed a phrase about himself and Wallace working together, remarking instead that Wallace was a personal friend; and abbreviated the commentary about how the Democratic party operated under a free convention system.

With the promise of a Roosevelt vote at the convention, which

Wallace was not going to get, and with advice to the delegates to choose their own candidate, Wallace had to be satisfied.

3

Byrnes proved just as difficult to control as Wallace, and again the president's refusal to say, himself, what the score was—that is, that the game was over and Byrnes had lost—caused much confusion.[56]

Byrnes was a sharp, alert individual who on many occasions had seized his opportunities. The diminutive, bright-eyed South Carolinian was a consummate political insider. For him to defy the president was perhaps easier than for Wallace, who doubtless did it out of principle. Byrnes did it out of sheer opportunity. Through the years he had enjoyed a remarkable career in which he fought his way upward, starting at near the bottom with a small local court post in 1908, and progressing from there to the House of Representatives in 1911, to the Senate in 1931, and the Supreme Court ten years later. In all his years in politics he made a single mistake, which was to accept the Supreme Court post; he discovered the court was a mausoleum, or so he told newspapermen who, having nothing else to do, sometimes walked out of the capitol building across First Street to the court building and talked idly with him. It is understandable why he got out of there the next year, into the White House as Roosevelt's principal assistant.

While in the White House the wily Byrnes pursued a course with the president that was wise as it could be: he constantly threatened the president with resignation. He may have done this out of pride, as he possessed a good deal of that. But he must have calculated it too, and it surely worked; the president seemed to respond better to outright threats than quiet loyalty. Senator Truman discovered this about the president during the 1930s, when he learned that voting a straight New Deal line did not endear him much to the president; Roosevelt passed all the Missouri patronage to his state's senior senator, Bennett Champ Clark, a charming drunk who did no work and voted erratically against Roosevelt. At the worst moment in Truman's political career, worse than the 1948 election, when in 1940 the governor of Missouri sought his Senate seat, Roosevelt intrigued with the governor against Truman—there was not an iota

of presidential gratitude. Roosevelt's assistant Harry Hopkins discovered this trait as well: for years he agreed with everything the
president said, did anything he wanted (it was said would jump off
the Washington Monument with or without parachute as the president desired), and as a reward never received a word of thanks, so he
later told Truman's press secretary, Charles G. Ross. James A. Farley,
former national chairman, who was out of the presidential circle from
1940 onward and admittedly irritable, wrote in his diary in 1946 that
he never received a single thank-you after 1930, when the then governor of New York for some reason thanked him for something.[57]

The president in the summer of 1944 had a special need for the
assistant president's services, and Byrnes knew it and took advan-
tage. Roosevelt was not going to attend the convention but would
only be passing through Chicago en route to San Diego. After ob-
serving troop maneuvers at Camp Pendleton he would board a heavy
cruiser and journey to Hawaii, to meet General Douglas MacArthur
and Admiral Chester W. Nimitz and decide which of the two com-
manders should dominate Pacific strategy: should it be MacArthur's
island-hopping or Nimitz's island-bypassing, this on the way to Tokyo? He would then take ship to Alaska and inspect installations—it
was midsummer—and come back by destroyer to the west coast.
During his absence he needed Byrnes in Washington, and he needed
Byrnes to not merely be there but to be there in fairly good spirits.

With everything calculated, on Tuesday, July 11, the day of the
leaders' conference, Byrnes made his move. He talked first to Hopkins, who understood how to approach the president on anything,
liked to be a kingmaker and to pull once in a while on the strings of
gratitude, and also, to change the figure, was a sort of sponge that
would absorb whatever liquid it came in contact with. Byrnes told
Hopkins he was a candidate if Roosevelt had no objection to his
candidacy. He thereupon saw Hannegan and Mayor Kelly, seeking to
advance his candidacy before the evening's meeting, only to discover
that they raised "the Negro question." What he said in reply is unknown, although one can guess he said he knew more about it than
his interlocutors. Late that afternoon he or his assistant, Walter
Brown, owner of a radio station in Spartanburg and a Byrnes intimate, "diverted" (to use the word Brown chose for his "log," or diary)
Walker into Byrnes's office just before the leaders assembled in the

east wing to go to the White House for dinner. According to Brown, who was either writing his log each evening or shortly thereafter, "JFB gives argument to Walker." What that was, he did not explain.[58]

If one were to draw Byrnes's fortunes the next day, Wednesday, on a graph, they would show a downward curve, then an upward one. At the outset he talked to Walker, at the same time Hannegan was seeing Wallace. Walker's talk was to tell Byrnes he had been "passed over." In talking with Byrnes he explained Roosevelt's message plainly. Brown's log gave Byrnes's response: "Walker called and urges JFB not to run. JFB argues with him." According to Walker, Byrnes was hurt, incredulous. In the early afternoon came information of a similarly disturbing sort from Hopkins, who that day lunched with the president. Hopkins asked the president who he thought would win the nomination if the convention was left free to choose. FDR promptly replied, "Byrnes." After this intelligence the president, according to Hopkins, subtracted from his praise and said, echoing Hannegan and Kelly, that the Negro question was acute. He said Byrnes would bring much support to the ticket but lose votes in states with large black populations. There could be less objection, he said, to Douglas. Hopkins raised the issue of the Catholic vote and Roosevelt, as he had told the leaders the night before, said he thought it no longer mattered.[59]

Nor was this all the discouraging information that day. Byrnes called his close friend, the head of the Foreign Economic Administration, Leo T. Crowley, and charged him with getting the president to change his mind. An intimate of Roosevelt, Crowley saw him that afternoon and heard about the Negro question. This question the president attributed to Flynn.

At that juncture matters improved. When Crowley left the oval office he went out through the east wing and stopped by Byrnes's office. The assistant president immediately went into action: "I got the President on the telephone and told him 'Leo is here in my office and has repeated his conversation with you. I would like to know if you have changed your opinion about my being a candidate.' The President said 'You are the best qualified man in the whole outfit and you must not get out of the race. If you stay in the race you are certain to win.'"[60]

Thursday, July 13, was similarly busy, and started when Byrnes

went to the president's office on official business, as he described it
years later; after Roosevelt disposed of the business, the president
said he wanted to talk politics. He told Byrnes, of course confiden-
tially, that he was having trouble with Wallace, who could not be
nominated but was insisting upon running unless the president told
him to withdraw. Knowing the president's way in such matters,
Byrnes agreed that the president could not tell the vice-president to
withdraw. Roosevelt explained his plan, which was to write Wallace
a lukewarm letter. "I had to do at least this for Wallace," he said.
"But don't you worry. Everyone assures me that you will be nominated without any trouble."[61]

Just what Byrnes said to the president during this colloquy is
difficult to be sure of, apart from his memoirs, though we do know in
detail what he told Brown afterward. If he put matters in the way
Brown wrote them down, it would have been a conference far more
sharp than it probably was. One can only suppose that the basic
ideas were bandied about but in more gentlemanly fashion. Even
though Byrnes was known as a straight-shooter, this was not the president's custom, and Byrnes had been around Roosevelt long enough to
understand that. According to Brown, Byrnes had gone over to see
the president for fifteen minutes and the conversation lasted an
hour. Ever the aggressor, Byrnes moved in on the president. When
Roosevelt said Byrnes would be nominated without any trouble, the
assistant president seized upon this revelation and said he hoped
Roosevelt would not express a preference for anyone else. Having
already done so, twice, the president said he would not do so. Byrnes
told Brown he also went for the Negro question, via the Catholic
question, by comparing what happened in 1940 to what might happen
four years afterward. "You told me a few weeks after the election that
the Catholic issue would not have mattered and you will be telling me
after this election that the Negro issue would not have mattered." He
showed the president a photograph he had just received from Aiken,
South Carolina, of Mrs. Roosevelt addressing a black audience. "Look
at the expression on their faces. That is idolatry. You can't tell me that
the fact you have a southerner on the ticket that those Negro people
are going to turn against Mrs. Roosevelt and the President who has
done more for them than anybody else in the history of the world."

"I believe you are right," was the presidential answer, to which

Roosevelt added he was only saying what Flynn and Mayor Kelly had told him: "All of us agreed you were the best qualified man and all of us would rather have you than anyone else, but they said they were afraid you would cost the ticket two or three hundred thousand Negro votes."

"Mr. President," Byrnes responded, "all I have heard around this White House for the last week is 'Negro.' I wonder if anybody ever thinks about the white people. Did you ever stop to think who could do the most for the Negro? This is a serious problem, but it will have to be solved by the white people of the South. If Mr. Wallace or Mr. Douglas says he is against the poll tax that is not news and they cannot change the views of southerners. But if I say I am against the poll tax, that means something."

The president interrupted that southerners had filibustered the anti-poll tax bill.

"Well," puffed Byrnes, "did Mr. Henry Wallace stop the filibuster? Do you think I could have stopped the filibuster if I had been the presiding officer of the Senate?"

"I believe you could have, Jimmy," said the president.

The conversation turned into badinage, with Roosevelt slyly adding another disqualification to Byrnes's list (he had dismissed—and thereby gently raised—the Catholic question, stressed the Negro question, and at the leaders' meeting on Tuesday there had been talk of the hold-the-line order). He ventured that Byrnes was too old. (Three years older than the president, Byrnes was sixty-five—born in 1879.) To which Byrnes responded that he had been working ten hours a day for the president and the only vacation he took was to go on a fishing trip with the president.

Before Byrnes left, Roosevelt added another discouraging thought: he said that at the leaders' meeting everyone believed Truman and Douglas would be the least objectionable candidates for vice-president. He balanced this news with another, his second, assurance that he would stand on his letter to Wallace and not deal any cards under the table.

Outside the office Byrnes espied the next presidential visitor, the vice-president of the Congress of Industrial Organizations, Sidney Hillman, who had come in through the east wing and escaped attention from newspapermen.

Between Byrnes and Hillman came Crowley, to impress on the

president how Byrnes was the best man. He told Roosevelt he had learned from the Republican standard-bearer in 1940, Wendell L. Willkie, that the latter would go for Roosevelt that fall if the Democrats did not run Wallace or Douglas. This was an important piece of information, for the president had been trying to divide the Republicans, presumably then conquering them, ever since the summer of 1940, when he had brought two premier Republicans, Henry L. Stimson and Frank Knox, into the cabinet as secretary of war and secretary of the navy, respectively. He had been working on Willkie, sending him around the world on a trip in 1942 that resulted in the book *One World* (1943). Willkie was a good man to have around, and it appeared as if Byrnes was the key to having him around.[62]

That afternoon the president called Crowley back into his office and said he did not want Byrnes to "feel badly toward me." He said he liked Jimmy better than anyone around the White House, that he did not want Byrnes to resign. During the conversation he told Crowley that Hannegan was going to write him a letter asking if he had any objection to Truman or Douglas and he was going to reply that he had none. Crowley, with a considerable gumption (according to Brown's log), said Roosevelt could not afford to do that because he would be taking sides, and the president shamefacedly admitted as much.

The day ended with a felicitous Hopkins touch.[63] Hopkins told Byrnes he believed the president wanted him to run, that both he, Hopkins, and FDR thought he could win. That evening the president left for Hyde Park.

On Friday, as on the preceding days, the skies momentarily darkened, and the agent of darkness was again Postmaster General Walker. Crowley had been busying himself attempting to "fix it with Byrnes," to use his phrase, and part of the effort involved arranging for Byrnes, Walker, and Hannegan to lunch with him in his suite at the Mayflower. As Walker recalled, "It was not a particularly happy meal." One subject was uppermost in the minds of the diners, the question of whether Roosevelt wanted Byrnes. Crowley kept shying away from it, and finally Walker lost patience and "pinned Crowley right down." "You told the president," he said, "and you told me you'd fix it with Byrnes. Why don't you tell Byrnes right here to his face that you know the president told me to tell him he was out?"[64]

Byrnes simply would not take "no" for an answer. What Crowley said at this juncture we do not know, but if it was what Walker asked him to say, Byrnes refused to take it seriously. According to Brown's log, admittedly secondhand but demonstrating what Byrnes remembered of this embarrassing luncheon, nothing of importance happened; all Walker and Hannegan did was try to convince him they were confused over what the president wanted done and were mostly concerned about preventing a split in the party during the convention. Byrnes pressed them for a statement that they would not do anything against him. Their answer was that if delegates asked them they would have to say that the president believed Byrnes would cost the ticket votes. Byrnes said he would carry this message back to Roosevelt, and if the latter confirmed what they said he would not be a candidate.[65]

Some of the above conversation, not all, appeared in Byrnes's autobiography, *All in One Lifetime,* published in 1958. Retired back to South Carolina, he sought to give the impression he had acted in gentlemanly fashion throughout, dealt with opponents fairly. Perhaps in the autobiography of a long life it is impossible to show nuances. But the governing nuance in his dealings with the president concerning his ambition for the vice-presidency (he might as well have said the presidency) was that Roosevelt was not going to tell him he was out. He knew Roosevelt well enough to know that. Walker, now accompanied by Hannegan, was again telling him the truth. He preferred to hedge an issue he thought he could force at the convention.

Nothing if not importunate, Byrnes went back to his office, wrote out a few questions he intended to ask the president, and telephoned him at Hyde Park. He took down the conversation in shorthand, and had a secretary on an extension do likewise.

The essence of the telephone call was over Walker's contention that the president preferred Truman or Douglas. Here Roosevelt resorted to outrageous subterfuge—which did not fool Byrnes but allowed him to continue the charade that the president really wanted him. "When we all went over the list," said the president, referring to the leaders' meeting, "I did not say that I preferred anybody or that anybody would cost me votes, but they all agreed that Truman would cost fewer votes than anybody and probably Douglas second. This was the agreement they reached and I had nothing to do with it. I was asking questions. I did not express myself." He told Byrnes that of all the people who had been mentioned for vice-president, he, Byrnes, was his closest friend.[66]

It was FDR at his duplicitous worst. Years later, in the autobiography, Byrnes published the conversation. He trimmed off a little, as it became repetitive. On the part of the president the repetition probably had a purpose, for it accentuated the doubts of Byrnes's candidacy he had set out before. In recalling the affair it was to Byrnes's interest not to display them. Even so, the conversation on Roosevelt's part was duplicitous, and Byrnes did demonstrate that.

Talking to Hannegan later that afternoon Byrnes read him the president's statement about "I was asking questions. I did not express myself." The chairman was an honest man, given if necessary to a little persiflage, but he had made his way in St. Louis politics and now in national politics by speaking the truth. He was dumbfounded, and said so. "Well," he responded, "I can't call the President a liar." He reiterated he was telling the truth.[67]

Byrnes did one other thing that Friday in the morning around 9:00 A.M. Washington time, well before the talks with Walker and Hannegan. He called Truman in Independence, and got him just as the senator was about to go out to the small barn behind the house at 219 North Delaware Street, get out his car, and leave for Chicago. "Harry," Byrnes said, "the President has given me the go sign for the Vice Presidency and I am calling up to ask if you will nominate me."[68]

Byrnes was trapping one of his principal opponents. In his autobiography he claimed, "I did not tell him that the President would support me."[69] That was a half-truth. When Truman in 1950 learned from Walker about his attempt, after the leaders' meeting, to tell Byrnes, on Wednesday and Friday, what the president wanted, Roosevelt's successor was angry. By that time he had broken with Byrnes over what he considered Byrnes's too independent stance as secretary of state in 1945–1947 and especially siding with the Dixiecrats in 1948, but he was now cognizant of a deeper disloyalty, this phone call to get him to nominate Byrnes. In a long, memorandum-like letter for the record, given to his close friend Press Secretary Ross, Truman, among other things, described Byrnes as a "slick conniver," which may not have been far from the mark.[70]

Tuesday, July 11, 1944, through Friday, July 14, had been a mo-

mentous time for Byrnes. Since Tuesday morning when he told Hopkins he was in the race if the president did not object, he had done
his best—with a thoroughness that would have been exemplary if
the purpose had been different—to pin the president down and to
arrange the opinions of anyone else who might thwart him. Given
the presidential outlook, he determined to overcome it. He may have
counted on the president's illness; one has the impression that both
he and Wallace counted on it, thinking it would reduce FDR's resis-
tance and together with their own labors allow them to shove aside
the president's contentions about their unavailability, getting the
issue into the convention where they could maneuver delegates and
achieve the nomination with all it meant for the presidency itself.

Byrnes came fairly close to success. What happened the next days,
over the weekend, gave evidence of that. Roosevelt's refusal to tell
him to his face he was out began to work in favor of the assistant
president.

In spite of Truman's later description of Byrnes as a slick conniver, Roosevelt, in 1944, was Byrnes's superior in the art of conniv-
ing. Arriving at Hyde Park from Washington on Friday morning, he
rested during much of the day—he was just getting up when Byrnes
called.[71] That evening he entrained for Chicago and points west. As
the train made its way across New York, Pennsylvania, Ohio, and
Indiana, he must have thought about what was necessary to stop his
two inconvenient vice-presidential candidates at the forthcoming convention. He had arranged to give Wallace a lukewarm endorsement,
which would do him no good. The question momentarily was Byrnes.
Indeed the president may already have thought about the Byrnes
problem: the previous Thursday he had talked with Hillman, just
after he was plying Byrnes with uncertainties about Negroes and
age. Hillman's visit offered opportunity to go back to what the leaders
had mentioned, labor's dislike of Byrnes. This dislike the president
might be able to convert into a fatal disqualification.

— 2 —

DECISION

Byrnes was so insistent, so pushing, that the first thing the president had to do was get him out of the race. As matters turned out, the next essential was to convince Truman to get into the race. These were the consuming enterprises of the next few days, between Saturday, July 15, and the following Wednesday, July 19, when the convention opened.

It again became clear how narrow a proposition was the fixing of the presidential choice on the senator from Missouri. The decision seemed to yawn one way, then the other.

Roosevelt always kept his decisions to himself. In this instance, however, the decision may have been so slow in coming, dangerously slow (Byrnes went to the convention determined to impose himself upon the delegates, and was likely to be good at that sort of thing), because the president was ill, in fact dying. It was difficult for him to give attention to the moves of the candidates. One has the impression that as much attention as he did bestow was almost putting him at the edge of his nervous energy.

1

Byrnes was the first problem, and after more confusion the president addressed the problem and got rid of it.

The confusion came when Hannegan, highly uncertain what the president wanted after Byrnes called Roosevelt at Hyde Park early Friday afternoon, began to believe Byrnes was to be the running mate. Years later Byrnes guessed that Hannegan's principal concern was to get Wallace out of the race, and this must have been true. Walker, a decade later, pondering the uneasy summer days of mid-

July 1944, believed Hannegan never was the Truman partisan he had been credited with being, and this also was probably true. A professional leader, no amateur, Hannegan looked at politics as coldly as he could; he liked, even admired, Truman, and would gladly have gone for him, but he would have taken almost anyone to get rid of Wallace. Moreover, he was like the other leaders in that he had to accept whatever choice Roosevelt made; it was hardly his own choice. After the convention there was a good deal of speculation, most of it unfriendly to Hannegan, that he had pushed his own man. This was totally untrue, for he was Roosevelt's chairman, not his own. That being the situation, and after listening to Byrnes, Hannegan decided that perhaps, after all, Byrnes was the right individual to solve the Wallace problem and that Roosevelt had decided likewise.[1]

McCullough has excoriated Hannegan for going over to Byrnes, as he considers it double-dealing. He has written that Hannegan was "playing an extremely deceitful game," and observes, too, that this was his first national convention.[2] He is unsure whether Roosevelt was behind Hannegan's action or not. But it is difficult to see how under the circumstances Hannegan could have done anything else.

The party chairman hence knew what he should do when he visited the president's train in the Fifty-first Street rail yard in Chicago that Saturday afternoon, July 15. He would ask the president point-blank if he, Roosevelt, wanted the convention to accept Byrnes. Then he would talk about Roosevelt's letter to Wallace, which was not yet quite to his, Hannegan's, pleasure—that is, it was still too friendly to Wallace. He would get a copy of that letter after, he hoped, he persuaded the president to make another change or so, toning it down. He also would get a copy of the letter on Truman that he had received only in penciled form; he would get that letter typed up on White House stationery.

The scene must have been strangely removed from anything Hannegan had experienced, almost eerie, as between 1:30 and 2:30 that Saturday afternoon, a warm summer day, with the temperature around eighty-six degrees, the national chairman of the party boarded the presidential train. One wonders what passed through his mind. It is possible nothing did—after all, he had been busy night and day, in Washington and now Chicago; he hardly had time to think. Still, he would have been lacking in imagination, which was something he possessed a great deal of, if he did not think a little about the scene he was looking at and what he was to learn from Roosevelt. The yard looked like any other big-city yard, tracks running parallel and sometimes moving into others, rails and ties stretching out in curious ways. It was a veritable maze. And within the maze lay the train of the most powerful political figure in the country, a man who had been president for more than eleven years and who was, himself, much like a spider at the center of a maze of his own making who could reach out and smite anyone who got in his way. What would the presidential spider do when Hannegan confronted him with questions and queries? Who was going to be president of the United States, after Roosevelt passed into history, his days coming to an end, illness taking its toll?

The train was being serviced. Apparently it had been traveling without an advance engine—the duty of the latter being to avert any security threats, such as taking the brunt of bombs along the tracks. There do not seem to have been any visible security measures, army contingents on hand, else a large body of Chicago policemen. The president's car, the *Ferdinand Magellan*, looked like an ordinary private car, but of course it was not. Built in 1929, one of a group of cars named for explorers, it had just been rebuilt and presented to the government by the country's leading rail lines. In its second incarnation it weighed 285,000 pounds, almost twice the weight of an ordinary Pullman, and was so heavy that a sizable charge of dynamite exploded directly under it would not budge it from the tracks. Its armor plate was five-eighths of an inch thick, including sides, roof, floor, ends of the car, and the doors. Window glass was three inches thick, and it could stop any bullet. The car was air- and watertight. All this for what in railroad parlance was known, as word of the train's passage was telegraphed along the right-of-way, as POTUS, that is, the train of the President Of The United States.

The chairman of the party, together with Mayor Kelly, clambered aboard. They found Mrs. Roosevelt and Judge Rosenman in the dining compartment with the president, finishing lunch. The president's wife and speechwriter excused themselves, leaving Hannegan and Kelly alone with "the boss."[3]

Hannegan did what he came to do. Reporters outside, who had followed him to the yard, timed his stay, which was fifty-two minutes.

He may have persuaded Roosevelt but much more likely was told by Roosevelt that Byrnes was an acceptable vice-presidential candidate. Mayor Kelly immediately afterward called Byrnes in Washington, with the presidential statement, "Well, you know Jimmy has been my choice from the very first. Go ahead and name him."[4]

Hannegan had to argue with the president to get the changes in the Wallace letter.[5] Roosevelt perhaps had tired of the letter and did not want to hear more of it. What Hannegan apparently did was persuade him to drop off the letter's latter half, which was a series of short paragraphs in the form of questions. The questions subtracted from the letter's most important point, which was that the delegates should decide on a candidate, that Roosevelt was not trying to dictate. Because they set out ideal qualities a vice-presidential running mate should possess, they gave the impression of instruction, that is, dictation. Lastly, one of the queries was embarrassing in a special way. "Will the nominee," it read, "meet the opposition in so-called doubtful states to the extent that he will diminish the strength of the ticket?" The question looked almost openly to the problem with the anti-Roosevelt Texas delegation. Pro-Roosevelt rump delegates were contesting its certification, trying to be helpful to the president, but in their zeal bringing public attention to the whole issue. Moreover, other southern delegations, notably those of Virginia and South Carolina, shared the anti-Roosevelt sentiments of the chosen Texans, and they were about to coalesce around the noncandidacy of the conservative Virginia senator Harry F. Byrd, the impossibly conservative head of the "Byrd machine," who voted Virginia as if he owned the state. Byrd, a diminutive, pinch-faced politico, grew apples in his orchards and sold them, and thought it would be possible to turn the United States into an apple orchard. He said he was not running for the presidency, and knew he had no chance, but naturally was pleased that his southern friends wanted to vote for him and did not really take himself out of the race by refusing votes. He knew he could be a small but conspicuous spoiler against the president's nomination.

Hannegan had the Truman letter typed up—for what use he was uncertain.

In faraway Washington, Jimmy Byrnes was sitting on the edge of his chair as he first anticipated the Hannegan-Roosevelt conversation—Kelly called him and said it was about to take place—and then got the happy news that the president was going over to him. In the words of the mayor of Chicago, "The President has given us the green light to support you and he wants you in Chicago."[6] Kelly said that when Byrnes arrived the next morning, Sunday, he should go right out to the mayor's Lake Shore Drive house and have breakfast with him and Hannegan.

After Hannegan set up things and Kelly made the second phone call, Byrnes repaired to Union Station. In preparation he decided to mask the reason for his attendance at the convention, which was a good idea, as he later would see. With reporters he avoided all questions relating to his availability for the vice-presidency and let them believe he was going as a member of the White House official family, to observe the events for the president.[7]

But as the enterprise began, Byrnes avoided one error only to make another. He asked for and obtained the biggest suite in the convention hotel, the Royal Skyway on the twenty-fourth floor of the Stevens. As his luck would have it, the suite had been reserved by Pauley, manager of the convention, for the delegation from his own state, California. Byrnes's act irritated the party treasurer no end. "I would not say," he remembered several years later, "that Byrnes used a wartime priority, but the urgent request of the Director of War Mobilization was sufficiently persuasive."[8] Pauley was no man to antagonize. Byrnes had not added a star to his crown.

Upon arrival in the city Byrnes sent Walter Brown to occupy the suite and climbed into the red automobile of the Chicago fire chief, to be whisked to Kelly's house where he found Hannegan bubbling over with enthusiasm that the president had gone back to Byrnes for vice-president. The three breakfasters put their minds to the task of organization, including signs reading "Roosevelt and Byrnes."

Arrangement for signs during the breakfast was another error. Some reporter must have had a representative among the sign makers, or the latter were talkers. Existence of the signs became known.

During the breakfast Hannegan mentioned to Byrnes a small issue, then no larger than a man's hand: the president had told him aboard the train to clear Byrnes's nomination with the CIO leaders, Hillman and the organization's president, Murray. Hannegan looked on this duty as a mere formality and so did Byrnes.[9]

After returning to the hotel Byrnes marshaled his many friends and acquaintances, and so did Hannegan, and put them to work. That evening the party leaders held a dinner for Byrnes at a north-side apartment "hangout" lent to Hannegan by a friend named Coston or Costigan. The dinner amounted to a victory celebration. Present were Kelly, Hannegan, Walker, and Byrnes's friend Crowley, who had accompanied Byrnes from Washington. Flynn of the Bronx was not present, as he was due in the next afternoon. During dinner Walker raised no objection to Byrnes, whose candidacy he had been trying to prevent. His position was exactly similar to that of the other leaders, namely, that although he preferred Truman he would be for whoever the president wanted; indeed, he said so that evening. The national committee's secretary, Allen, had gone out to Chicago with Walker and wrote afterward, "We still didn't know, when we got there, whom the President finally would pick for the Vice-Presidential nomination. We thought it would be Truman, but we couldn't be sure. Roosevelt could, of course, have named anybody."[10] At the end of the gathering, as Byrnes remembered, while everyone was standing and about to leave, Hannegan turned to Kelly and said, so as to relate the fact to the others present, who had not been in attendance at the breakfast, "Ed, there is one thing we forgot. The President said, 'Clear it with Sidney.'"[11]

In retrospect it is difficult to know how far Byrnes could have gone with his ambitions beyond the position he occupied that Sunday evening—celebrating with his newfound friends around the dinner table in the northside apartment, returning to the Stevens in triumph accompanied by Crowley, and there regaling him and Brown over what had happened—had it not been for "Clear it with Sidney." It is possible that opposition might have developed in other ways, for Byrnes had made a fair number of enemies. Taking the Skyway suite was typical of him. Someone, some group, might yet have tried to throw a monkey wrench into his plans, slip a shoe into the machinery.

One has the impression that Byrnes could have taken the nomination, had it not been for the president's admonition to Hannegan, and maybe even despite it. For the rest of his long life—Byrnes and Truman died the same year, 1972—he could wonder whether he might have ignored the clearance Roosevelt wanted, taken his fight for the nomination to the floor, marshaled every single friend and supporter, including many, many individuals in the South, and made such a showing against Wallace that the president in weariness would have given in, wishing to avoid the spectacle of the party torn to shreds over a vice-presidential nomination. The president might have sighed and said again that "Jimmy" had been his choice from the very first, go ahead and name him.

By opposing Roosevelt and taking the nomination, Byrnes could have made a decision that would have changed American history—a southern president in the immediate postwar period might have championed the racial positions he mentioned to Roosevelt as possible, coming out against the poll tax and in favor of a Fair Employment Practices Committee, supporting the civil rights movement before it took on far larger proportions and turned violent. In short, President Byrnes might have headed off much of the racial discord that has haunted American life and politics throughout the latter half of the century.

As matters turned out, if indeed the moment was there for Byrnes to seize, if he could have arranged the vice-presidential nomination despite the president's injunction about Hillman, he did not rise to the occasion. The dinner at the apartment therefore marked the apogee of his political fortunes. Like his appointment to the Supreme Court, though the stakes were far higher, he made another mistake in his political career. He would go on to a very considerable public service, for Truman asked him to be secretary of state the next year, after Roosevelt's funeral, to take effect as soon as the new president could get Secretary of State Edward R. Stettinius, Jr.—an impossible occupant of that important post because he was a real lightweight—out of office. Byrnes took over the state department just after the end of the San Francisco conference that founded the United Nations Organization. He was secretary of state from July 1945 until January 1947, at the very beginning of the cold war era, and engaged in some of the most fateful international conferences of the present century, during which it might have been possible—no one will ever know—to have prevented the cold war. After his resignation, offered and accepted because he believed, erroneously, that his heart would not take the strain of continued public office, he retired back to South Carolina, where he soon was active in the politics of his native state as governor and leader of southerners just a shade removed from the racial intransigences of the Dixiecrats, who opposed Truman in the presidential election of 1948. Out of office in the mid-1950s, he remained in Columbia and wrote his memoirs. He must have ruminated over what had happened, welcoming visits from his friend Brown, who lived in Spartanburg and could drive over to reinforce his feelings of intense disappointment in the way the political ball had bounced. He must have believed that just a little more pushing at Chicago would have resolved everything.

Did Byrnes have some reason for not putting up a fight at Chicago? It is difficult to believe he lost his nerve. Was there a private reason? The *New York Times* reporter Turner Catledge, himself a southerner, was present at Chicago and writing his paper's lead stories. He was drawn to Byrnes and must have talked things over with him, then and later. Years afterward he published a charming autobiography in which he admitted the succession Roosevelt-Truman was what the country needed, that Byrnes had allowed himself to become too much of a southerner, but he ventured an interesting possibility. He wrote that Byrnes lost the great prize because of his wife, "Miss Maude," to whom he was devoted. Byrnes, Catledge said, did not want the religious issue brought out in public, as it surely would have been, because it would have embarrassed Miss Maude.[12]

The turn away from Catholicism to Episcopalianism, and what Byrnes's wife would have thought when it was written up, may have been the rock on which Byrnes's hopes were dashed, although it does not seem plausible. Despite Catledge's astuteness it seems like a Victorian explanation, unbelievable considering what was at issue. Byrnes's wife could have put up with a little public criticism and must already have known, probably well indeed, what it was to be the wife of a prominent political figure.

For a reason that defies analysis Byrnes's moment passed, within a single day, between Sunday evening and Monday evening, July 16–17, 1944. The way in which it disappeared was not at first visible. On Monday morning he was up bright and early and over to the Blackstone Hotel, across a virtual alley, Balboa Street, from the Stevens, where he ensconced himself in the room next to Hannegan, who was on the seventh floor corner, rooms 708–709. When he arrived the party chairman was just getting up and was again full of enthusiasm, sure the movement for Roosevelt and Byrnes was underway. The sign makers would be busy that day; all was in order. He had asked Byrnes to take the room next door, number 710, so he could work closely with him, watching over his candidacy, sweeping away obstacles as they appeared.

Two obstacles then turned up, and taken together spelled the end of Byrnes's candidacy. One was the opposition that developed over Roosevelt's incidental (as it seemed) injunction, "Clear it with Sidney." The other was marked by the arrival of Flynn that afternoon and the latter's continuing concern, as he described it, about losing two hundred thousand Negro votes in New York, throwing the state's electoral votes to Dewey, together with loss of black votes elsewhere, such as in Chicago, with possible loss of Illinois to the Republicans, indeed loss of the whole election—all this in case Byrnes were the candidate.

The CIO issue was far more serious and, as the *New York Times* bureau chief in Washington, Arthur Krock, present in Chicago, revealed a few days after the convention, probably decisive. Krock had some facts wrong, and did not know the maneuvering that accompanied the preliminaries to and course of the convention, but he was right about what labor in the person of Sidney Hillman did to Byrnes.[13]

The situation was easy to understand. The distinguished biographer of Roosevelt, Frank Freidel, has written that labor generally and Hillman particularly were important to the president in the election, for many servicemen were out of the country, others in strange places, and most of them Roosevelt supporters. Too, many war workers were in new localities, and registration to vote was not easy.[14] If the president could not marshal labor he might be in real trouble. As for Hillman, he was an emigrant from Lithuania who had gotten his start in the Chicago pants-cutting industry, removed to New York where he became a successful organizer, founded the Amalgamated Clothing Workers of America, became vice-president of the CIO, and, together with his co-worker Murray, used his boundless energies to take the CIO to a position of virtual equality with the cautious, staid American Federation of Labor. He had an eye for the main chance, and during the war when union strength had grown he took on a political role, joining the government for a while as co-director of the Office of Production Management, then organizing a political action committee—the latter differing in many ways from the committees of later (and present) vintage, its principal purpose being voter mobilization, not the canvassing of monetary support.

At Chicago there was no question that labor was for Wallace. To Hillman and Murray, Wallace was the ideal candidate; Wallace's idea of a Century of the Common Man attracted them. Wallace, in turn, had courted labor.

But the question for labor at Chicago became initially one of who not to be for. On Monday, July 17, labor in the person of Hillman chose to display its muscle against Byrnes, who to the CIO vice-president was an impossible candidate for vice-president of the U.S. Byrnes had held the line and that was too heavy a burden—he could not carry it into the vice-presidency. It was as simple as that. Or so it seemed. At first everything appeared all right. Byrnes said he would not talk to Hillman but would see Murray, and saw him at 3:00 that afternoon. Murray said labor was for Wallace, but he personally would not oppose Byrnes. Whereupon he left. What Byrnes did not know was that when Murray went back to see Hillman, the latter seems to have objected violently.

The possibility must have crossed Byrnes's mind that Monday in Chicago, as he waited in the room in the Blackstone, that the president had used Hillman to veto his candidacy. If it did not cross his mind that Monday morning it surely did later. As he ruminated in days and weeks to come he became bitter about it, and indeed never forgot it for the rest of his long life. The president, he believed, slipped a knife into his back, all the while smilingly—he imagined the scene—conversing with Hannegan in the rail yards and impressing the chairman with how friendly he was toward him. He had seen Hillman waiting outside the oval office the preceding Thursday—just before Roosevelt lunched with Wallace and, Byrnes believed, undertook to knife Wallace too. Wallace would receive a presidential letter. That was a better way to go than to deal with Hillman. For a professional whose experience went back to the presidency of William H. Taft, to be done in by an amateur, a man who had been in politics only a year or two, was terribly humiliating.

There is no proof, however, that the president used Hillman this way. It would have been much like him; Roosevelt was accustomed to work either through party leaders like Hannegan and Walker or amateurs who wittingly or unwittingly took assignments. One single source, Ickes's diary, contains two tantalizing testimonies, one from Rosenman, the other from Hillman, that state that when the labor leader saw Roosevelt the preceding Thursday the president told him what to do, or if the president did not tell him then he got word to him in time to get Byrnes out of the vice-presidential race. Rosenman told Ickes, "It had been necessary to rely upon Hillman to lay down the law as to Byrnes." Hillman himself, friendly with the diarist, told him that "the President stopped that nomination" through him. The only trouble with these testimonies is that both were after the fact, after Truman's nomination, and perhaps resembled the constant efforts of Hopkins to get on the winning side. The truth is that we really do not know, beyond his personal feeling about holding the line, why Hillman turned against Byrnes.[15]

In what now seems to have been the lesser reason for the destruction of Byrnes's candidacy, the black vote in New York City and elsewhere, it is equally possible that Roosevelt put Flynn up to raising the issue. Flynn might even have suggested it to Roosevelt, as he had reason (as we will see) to feel irritated with Byrnes. But again we do not know.

What does seem clear is that in raising the issue of the black vote Flynn was a good deal less important than he claimed in his charmingly exaggerated memoir. Byrnes, in *All in One Lifetime,* believed that Flynn, no less than Hillman, did him in. McCullough has gone along with this belief and indeed made Flynn the hero of his chapter on the Chicago convention. Still, it all seems improbable. Flynn's appearance at a national committee meeting on Monday afternoon and at a leaders' meeting early in the evening simply underlined what already was becoming clear: if the leaders continued to push Byrnes and the latter did not have the labor vote they could bring on a floor fight in which Wallace might win. They were none too sure of Roosevelt's championship of Byrnes, anyway. It was time to find out where everyone had to stand.

Flynn's role was to raise the need for clarification.[16] For what his opinions were worth that crucial Monday, he recited them, apparently not at once that afternoon when he came into the committee meeting but, according to his autobiography, early that evening when the leaders got together at Hannegan's suite in the Blackstone. When he arrived in the afternoon Hannegan rushed him over to a corner and said, "It's all over. It's Byrnes." Flynn said that could not be, that Roosevelt was for Truman. Hannegan said Kelly had agreed to go for Byrnes. Flynn thought to himself that Kelly hoped for a deadlock as he could put over the Illinois senator Scott Lucas. The latter name had not arisen on anyone's list thus far, and does seem hardly possible, but so Flynn wrote three years later. Flynn did not make any point that afternoon, but when he was in Hannegan's suite later, together with Hannegan and Walker, he does seem to have protested. Walker remembered that the gloves were off; to Flynn, everything was simple: "The boss wanted Truman, and Truman was the man."[17] According to Flynn he did more than that: he threatened, shouted, and swore. But it is doubtful that he made as much of a ruckus as he claimed. To carry on in front of some small political fish in the Bronx or Manhattan would have been one thing, but to try such a scene with two hardened types like Hannegan and Walker was ludicrous. They could have listened to him, tolerated the explosion, sensed that on the sleeper from New York he might not have gotten his beauty sleep. They could have guffawed. Flynn's importance was, again, to clarify. Walker, who was far more important in the equation, saw immediately that it was necessary to call Roosevelt and get things straightened out. Walker remembered that he could not be for Truman unless Byrnes was out; with Byrnes still in the race such a course would have been suicidal, dividing the conservative vote. All Wallace needed was a bare majority; after the 1936 Democratic convention the old two-thirds rule, by which any successful candidate needed a two-thirds vote, had been abandoned.

Byrnes afterward, quite erroneously, constructed an elaborate scenario in which Flynn moved against him.[18] It all started, Byrnes calculated, when Flynn surreptitiously had gotten the New York City street commissioner or some such dignitary to send a quantity of paving blocks out to his house, where he used them to improve his driveway. Reporters found out about this indiscretion and the affair became known as the Paving Block Incident. President Roosevelt, who did not mind a shenanigan of this sort, took pity on Flynn and decided he should have an ambassadorship to improve his image, and proposed to send him to China. Byrnes, in conference with Roosevelt, asked, "What qualifications does he have for that particular assignment?" In a fit of honesty the president replied, "None." The arrangement was to have the president's "missus" talk with Mrs. Chiang Kai-shek, who was coming on one of her trips to the United States, and she would demur over Flynn's appointment and it would fail. Perhaps the president himself would have talked with the wife of the president of China; Mrs. Chiang was a curvaceous lady who flirted with anyone, and Roosevelt doubtless enjoyed her visits; he could have told her exactly what she was to say so as to resolve Flynn's problem, which she would have enjoyed, for she liked political maneuvering as well as flirting. Not long afterward the president decided to send Flynn to Australia. At this juncture Byrnes had become too prominent. He was present at a meeting of several senators with the candidate, during which Flynn decided to withdraw.

The Chinese and Australian episodes, following upon the Paving Block Incident, were almost too trivial to analyze, and surely their consequences were less than Byrnes imagined; the South Carolinian had been in politics too long and could see intrigue everywhere. He seems to have believed that his part in the Chinese matter had gotten back—that Roosevelt probably told Flynn that Byrnes objected. The president probably did; he would not have missed the opportunity. But on such a national issue in 1944 as choosing a vice-presidential nominee for the party, with the prospect, as Flynn knew, that the nominee would become president, it is impossible to believe he would have acted against Byrnes out of pique. It made no more sense than that Byrnes would give up the presidency for fear of embarrassing his wife over Episcopalianism.

What Flynn did when closeted with Hannegan and Walker that late Monday afternoon at the Blackstone was to provoke a phone call to the president's train, and the leaders made it at 6:45 that evening. The three leaders went on the line separately to the president, answering questions and explaining Byrnes's two major disqualifications—of which refusal of Hillman and Murray to agree to his candidacy was much more important than Flynn's point. Actually during the past week the president perhaps had told Byrnes that he, Roosevelt, knew more about the Negro question than Flynn and Kelly. Moreover, Byrnes, on Sunday, the day before, had talked to Congressman William Dawson of Chicago, the sole black member of the House of Representatives, and Dawson said he did not think blacks would leave the party because of Byrnes.[19]

When the leaders talked to the president the issue of Byrnes's candidacy was immediately resolved. Roosevelt and everyone else knew exactly what had to be done. Walker went on the phone last. "Frank," said Roosevelt, "go all out for Truman."[20]

In accord with Rooseveltian practice ("that was the way the game was played"), a notification by someone other than the president was in order, and the group thoughtfully delegated Byrnes's friend Crowley to tell the assistant president he could not be vice-president. The words Crowley transmitted, and they must have been Roosevelt's, were that for the ticket Byrnes would be a "political liability."[21]

It was the end. Walter Brown, present when the messenger arrived, wrote that the news "knocked JFB cold." According to the faithful Brown, "His face flushed and it was apparent that this statement from the man he had served politically so faithfully cut him to the quick."[22] The greatest possibility of a lifetime vanished into thin air.

Brown wrote that the three of them—Byrnes, Crowley, himself—went to bed that night convinced all was lost. But given Byrnes's propensity to call Roosevelt when he wanted to know something, it was only to be expected he would do just that. Brown called the White House operator in Washington and arranged for the president to talk to Byrnes the next morning, catching the president when his train made a station stop.

McCullough has written that when Byrnes tried to call the president on Tuesday morning, Roosevelt refused the call. This was not true; Truman made that assertion to Jonathan Daniels in 1949, but he had no way of knowing. The call went right through, and the president was charming to the man he had just shoved out of the vice-presidential race. Byrnes came out in the open, asking if Roosevelt had said he would be a political liability. The president denied it. He said (and Byrnes must have been taking the words down in shorthand),

I did tell them yesterday what I told you—the same thing—that Wallace had his liabilities on account of a certain element among the voters. This was four or five days ago—and you did too, and there still remains the four things they cited as objections. I have not talked to anyone except yesterday when I repeated what I had told you. I told Flynn yesterday I had to agree with his estimate of the situation; that is, at long range. I have not seen anybody since I left home.[23]

The president confirmed what Byrnes knew was a possibility, that the proposed Truman letter was no piece of theory but had gone to Hannegan. "The only thing I told Bob was to show you a letter I wrote to Bob on that assumption—it was in reply to a question from Bob; he wanted confirmation of the fact that I would be entirely happy with Truman or Douglas. This was a week ago. It was in reply to a question from him."[24]

It was an irony, but the notion that Hannegan asked the president a question was not merely unbelievable but was a device Byrnes had invented for, now, his own discomfiture. When Roosevelt had cast about for some diplomatic way to announce his candidacy for a fourth term, Byrnes told him to write a letter in response to a nonexistent inquiry from Hannegan. The president wrote the letter. ("Dear Mr. Hannegan: You have written me that in accordance with the records a majority of the delegates have been directed to vote for my re-nomination for the office of President, and I feel that I owe to you, in candor, a simple statement of my position. . . .") He dated it July 10 and gave it out at a press conference the same day, and it was published the next day.[25] A week later he turned this device against Byrnes.

Byrnes wrote years afterward that if he had known of the letter to Hannegan he would have withdrawn, unless Roosevelt had written a similar letter to him.[26] This was an afterthought. The president told Crowley the preceding Thursday he was going to write a letter, so Byrnes expected it. The brave talk in *All in One Lifetime* did not occur, could not have occurred during the conversation with the president on Tuesday morning, July 18.

On the telephone Byrnes was reduced to a momentary hope that if he could remove the stigma that he was antilabor he might change the president's mind. He said he talked to Murray the day before, who said if Wallace would not be nominated the CIO would be disappointed but would support the president regardless of who was nominated, that the CIO had no other place to go.

This reminded Roosevelt that after the leaders called him the evening before, they were to have dinner with Hillman and Murray, and he wondered what they talked about.

Byrnes, incidentally, afterward forgot the presidential query and became sure that Hillman and Murray, especially Hillman, took part in the Monday evening phone conversation. In his memoirs he asserted this point as fact.

On Tuesday afternoon Hannegan came over to see Byrnes to reiterate what Crowley said. Byrnes told him the president denied he had described Byrnes as a political liability. As happened a few days before, Hannegan again was aghast. With "great earnestness" he said "that if he never saw his children again he would have to say that it was the exact truth and that if the President denied it to him, he would have to resign and would do so before he would withdraw it." He told Byrnes about the Truman letter and said every time he brought up Byrnes's name at the White House conference Roosevelt turned thumbs down; hence, he wanted the letter to put over Truman. After the Saturday conference he thought seriously of tearing up the letter but decided to keep it.[27]

At 3:00 that afternoon, Byrnes saw Alexander F. Whitney, president of the Brotherhood of Railroad Trainmen, the big AFL union. Al Whitney was a Byrnes man. He had talked with Hillman that morning and Hillman reiterated that the CIO would not take Byrnes.[28]

Whether the Whitney conversation came before or after that with Hannegan is not clear, but it did not matter, for Byrnes told Hannegan he would withdraw but would hold off on a statement until he could talk with Kelly, who had been friendly and helpful. Late that evening Kelly came over and the two talked for more than an hour. He confirmed what Hannegan said and related he would have to go for Truman. Both agreed that Roosevelt would not tell the truth and "stay hitched on political matters," that he was "warm-hearted in everything but politics and there he was cold-blooded." Kelly said he was the only man he had ever known in politics "who would stay at the top and not keep his word."[29]

2

Once the president decided—really decided—on Truman, the next order of business for the leaders was to convince the Missouri senator he was the president's choice; this took almost two days, Monday evening until Wednesday afternoon. Truman naturally was wary, and then, as it turned out, had other reasons for hesitating about the nomination.

That Truman knew the finger of destiny was beginning to point toward him is perfectly clear, for he had had plenty of warnings over the past several months and especially the last few days. His problem was to separate the enthusiasm of the warners from what he sensed was a rapidly changing reality. Hannegan called him after the leaders' meeting of July 11—he was in Kansas City—and told him what was decided; Truman told two close Missouri friends, "Bob Hannegan says he's going to make me Vice President."[30] But when people told him the president wanted him, how could he know? He was aware of the president's inconstancy: whatever Roosevelt's strengths, and no one could be unaware of them, the president often found it difficult to remember who his friends were. Roosevelt in 1940 had conspired with Stark, all the while claiming to be neutral in the Missouri Senate race; his hatchet man, Press Secretary Early, announced publicly that the president never took part in primary contests. Moreover, Truman knew that at the convention many people, notably Byrnes and Wallace, also Barkley, and a dozen favorite sons, were trying for the nomination. He must have felt that since not all could win there were certain to be disappointments. Byrnes doubtless was only the first candidate to fail. He had no desire to be one of the others.

And so Truman took a stance that he was not in the race, and when people inquired he told them so. He said this to the publisher of the *Kansas City Star,* Roy Roberts, on Thursday, July 13, and afterward wrote his wife about it—Bess then being in Denver visiting her brother. He did not like Roberts, who not only was a Republican and a hugely fat man who could order a steak for dinner, with all the trimmings, and then order another steak, but also, together with his newspaper, had been critical of the senator over the years. Roberts obviously wanted to be a kingmaker, and Truman would have none of it, giving him a "tough interview," saying "I didn't want the Vice Presidency." He had telephone calls from West Virginia and Oklahoma delegates and told them to vote for Barkley. The California delegation was in confusion; when Senator Sheridan Downey called, Truman said he did not want California's votes (although he knew Downey could not have delivered them). Before he left for the convention he went across the street in Independence to see his aged Aunt Ella, who lived at 216 North Delaware with her two spinster daughters, Ethel and Nellie. Ethel remembered that he said, "Aunt

Ella, I'm going to the convention to defeat myself; I don't want to be Vice President."[31]

Arriving at the convention, he said the same thing to Ed Harris of the *Post-Dispatch*. "I've thought it over very carefully," he told Harris, on Sunday evening, July 16. "And I'm not a-gonna do it. You know I'm not afraid of a fight. I'm sure I could win the nomination and be vice-president. But what then?" He was having a drink with Harris and studied his amber-hued glass as if, Harris wrote, "it were a crystal ball." "You and a lot of other friends tell me I might inherit the presidency and write my chapter of history. Well, the plain fact is, I don't want to be president." He looked up expectantly. "You want to know why?" The senator told Harris that for both personal and historical reasons he had decided not to be a candidate. During any campaign he would be vilified for his old Pendergast connections. His wife, daughter, and ninety-year-old mother were involved, and though he himself had a thick skin and could "take it," he did not think it would be fair to ask his family to take it. Besides, he was happy in the Senate. As for the historical part of the equation, if anything happened to Roosevelt and he succeeded to the White House he would soon be assailed as "incompetent," a "little man trying to fill big shoes." He ticked off the names of vice-presidents who through fate found themselves presidents—Tyler, Fillmore, Andrew Johnson, Arthur. There were notable exceptions such as Theodore Roosevelt. He did not mention Coolidge. Failure, frustration, and ridicule had attended almost all of these accidental presidents. "Forget it," he said. "I've already told Bob Hannegan and the others that I'm completely out of it. And I'm going to place Jimmy Byrnes' name in nomination."[32]

Setting about the business of getting support for Byrnes, the senator must have felt momentarily as if he were on a bandwagon—Byrnes's cause looked good on Saturday and Sunday, even as late as Monday morning. From all accounts Truman was moving among the delegates at this time, plumping for Byrnes. He had composed his nominating speech, and read it to Byrnes.

It is an interesting question when he realized that developments at the convention, while still complicated, were beginning to move in his direction. One has the feeling it was somewhat earlier than his memory of what happened.

According to his own story he was unimpressed when after the

Monday night telephone call Hannegan came to say that he, Truman, was the president's choice. After all, other people so often had been told the same thing, by Roosevelt himself, only to be disappointed. Talking to Daniels in 1949 he remembered saying to Hannegan, "Tell him to go to hell. I'm for Byrnes." He claimed to have offered another historical explanation: "'Bob, look here I don't want to be Vice President. I bet I can go down on the street and stop the first ten men I see and that they can't tell me the names of the last ten vice presidents of the United States. I bet you can't tell me who was McKinley's vice president.' He couldn't and that one became President of the United States. By golly, he couldn't."[33]

Behind that explanation one must suspect that when he received word from Hannegan he knew at once what had happened. Roosevelt had changed his mind again—the president had opted for Truman at the leaders' meeting, then gone to Byrnes, and was back to Truman. If Byrnes was out, this meant that whoever the president chose, and it apparently was Truman, would represent conservative delegates at the convention against liberal delegates pledged or friendly to Wallace. If the conservatives won, he would have the nomination. But he could not afford to get excited; the president could change his mind once more. We do not know his reaction, beyond what he remembered telling Hannegan in 1949, which probably was apocryphal, as it was what he had told Harris. We do not even know for certain if Hannegan talked to him Monday night or Tuesday. It seems impossible the party chairman would have let the evening go by without talking to him.

The next morning, Tuesday, he breakfasted with Hillman in the latter's suite at the Ambassador East Hotel. According to his own account he asked Hillman to endorse Byrnes, and Hillman refused, saying labor was for Wallace, but if it became necessary to go for someone else there was another man labor could be for and "I'm looking at the other one."[34]

This was the moment! Not before, surely, and certainly not later, as Truman claimed. He was receiving fascinating new information. He could not be sure what a presidential endorsement meant. If support for Truman did not appear, the unreliable president might endorse someone else. But along with an endorsement the support of labor could put him over.

He would have been a fool—a damned fool, he would have said—not to understand what Hillman was saying. He had enough presence of mind to make the right response: "I said I was not running and that Byrnes was my man."

What moved Hillman to such a statement? It was one thing to do in Byrnes, and another to sponsor Truman. But as the question of whether the president "programmed" him for the former action has never been answered conclusively, so with his preference for Truman. He already was suffering from the cardiovascular disease that would kill him two years later; he would not live long enough to write the memoirs that might have revealed why he spoke to Truman this way at breakfast in his suite in Chicago. Unlike Hannegan, he seems to have been a loner; he did not have confederates such as Walker to fill in the details of the story.[35]

Hillman had seen Roosevelt the preceding Thursday, and this raises the interesting possibility that the president and Hillman struck two deals during their conversation, not merely one against Byrnes, but also one in favor of Truman. The president would not have been above such dealing, nor would Hillman; both were schemers. Murray thought his assistant quite possibly made a deal in favor of Truman, that he and the president "cooked up" a second choice. Just after Hillman saw the president he and Murray held a news conference in Washington, in which they announced Wallace as their first choice. Reporters noticed that Hillman tried to name a second choice but Murray interrupted and said labor had no second choice. Murray later told Wallace that Hillman was about to name Truman. Hillman told Murray the following Monday, "We must have a second choice." (That same day a spokesman for the CIO said the group had no second choice.)[36]

For Roosevelt to deal with Hillman, however, was unlikely. It would have been out of character. He did not know Hillman well. All the talk about "Sidney" was the president's way; he called everyone by his or her first name, save General George C. Marshall, to whom he did it just once, to Marshall's obvious displeasure. Besides, he preferred to hold his cards. It is likely that he measured Hillman, inquiring to himself how he could use him. He knew from Ickes, who had wormed it out of Hillman, that the latter would take anyone for the nomination the president would suggest.[37] He thus learned that although Hillman would balk over Byrnes he would not balk to the end; he might therefore have stiffened Hillman with a little friendly badinage about how Byrnes could not possibly get the nomination. He must have been unsure if the AFL (which disliked Wallace and was neutral on an alternative candidate) was strong enough to offset the CIO. While listening to Hillman he may have made a mental note that it would be well to endorse Byrnes, perhaps on Saturday when he saw Hannegan, and see how far he, Byrnes, could go. That would allow him to hold back his decision for Truman. He did not like to do anything, take any course, before he had to; no politician likes to do that. Moreover, he was tired—tired of all the pressure from Byrnes and Wallace, tired for another reason he did not understand.

In the realm of deals it is possible that Hillman, if uninstructed for Truman on Thursday or afterward, made a personal deal during his breakfast with Truman. A recent biographer of Hillman, Steven Fraser, strongly suspects that for months the head of the CIO's political action committee had been planning what to do in case Wallace lost. That seems likely. Hillman's earlier biographer, Matthew Josephson, who knew many of Hillman's friends, claimed matters went so far that Hillman arranged to see Truman in New York at the apartment of the general counsel for the Amalgamated Clothing Workers of America, Maxwell Brandwen, on Sunday, July 9; but Truman perhaps thought the idea too dangerous, in view of his stance of not being a candidate, and told Hillman he would see him at the convention. In Chicago, at the breakfast, Josephson claimed a deal or if not that then "a pretty clear understanding" and attributed his proofs "according to accounts preserved by Hillman's intimates." According to Josephson the CIO's friends at the convention would fight for Wallace, but when Wallace's progress was checked then the swing to Truman would come on. Hillman, he wrote, feared Truman would move up too fast. The role of the CIO would be as a reserve against any thrust for Byrnes or some other "reactionary."[38]

Actually the idea of a personal deal is not as far-fetched as it might seem. It is clear that Hillman at Chicago was not working closely with the president of the CIO. Unlike Murray, Hillman surely sensed how Wallace had lost Roosevelt's favor and knew Truman would be a much better bet, or at least a second bet. Well aware of Murray's loyalty to Wallace—Murray had embarrassed him publicly on this score—he may have been following the time-honored course of *sauve qui peut*. After the political leaders made their telephone call to Roosevelt and followed it with a dinner with Hillman and Murray, and knowing Hillman's modest enthusiasm for the then vice-president, they may have tipped him off as to whom the president wanted, allowing him to get on the winning side. At the dinner they did not tell Murray, who in 1948 confided to a close friend of Truman, Max Lowenthal, that as late as Wednesday afternoon he had no idea the leaders had gone back to Truman. At the dinner Hannegan proposed to Hillman and Murray, "We will withdraw Jimmy Byrnes if you will withdraw Wallace."[39] That was a slyness; the president already had withdrawn Jimmy; Hannegan was bidding from nothing, hoping to see what cards the labor leaders would put on the table. After this ploy one of the political leaders may have told Hillman what was about to happen. Propriety would have dictated that Hillman afterward tell Murray, but if in fact he obtained such knowledge he did not impart it; he may have decided to let Murray, who had opposed him in the Washington news conference, go down with Wallace's ship. The president of the CIO stayed with Wallace to the end and paid a very high price for his loyalty, in terms of later influence at the White House. On Wednesday afternoon, immediately after Truman decided to run, Lowenthal arranged a meeting between Truman and Murray and picked up Truman at the Blackstone and drove him over to the Morrison. There Murray held out for Wallace. "I think you should not be a candidate for vice president," he told Truman. The latter's response was, "I do not want to be. I have been drafted. Goodbye, Phil." The candidate emerged from the Morrison in about two minutes, and thereafter his relations with the president of the CIO were cool indeed until November 2, 1948, when Truman's election, which Murray enthusiastically supported, changed everything.[40]

All of which allows a speculation that Hillman, by supporting Truman at the outset of the Chicago convention, may have undercut Murray in hope of taking Murray's place as head of the CIO. Early in 1945, Roosevelt's secretary of labor, Frances Perkins, became completely disillusioned with Hillman when the latter told her he was turning against Roosevelt. She stayed after a cabinet meeting and informed FDR of what Hillman said, and the president allowed as to how the labor leader possessed a big head. A decade later, undertaking an enormous (and enormously frank) oral history, she was still angry: "He was neither reliable nor loyal. . . . I mean to me, the President, to his friends, to anything."[41]

As mentioned, when Hillman had breakfast with Truman, Tuesday morning, July 18, 1944, the labor leader confirmed what the senator probably had learned from Hannegan the night before (and Hillman, too, learned from Hannegan or one of Hannegan's confederates), that he, Truman, was one of the two principal candidates, considering that Byrnes was out.

Just to keep everyone on his toes, Murray and Hillman that same day, Tuesday, declared in an interview with James A. Hagerty of the *New York Times* that they had one candidate and only one candidate, Wallace. "They insisted that they were not considering anybody else for second place on the ticket and that, if someone else should be nominated, the CIO committee would meet again and decide what to do." The next day, Wednesday, when Hillman saw Wallace privately (for which see below), he denied he had said anything on behalf of Truman.[42]

Meanwhile Truman was mulling over several awkward considerations about the nomination that he had not thought much about. He had not turned them in his mind, attempting to resolve their importance, because the nomination had not seemed close enough.

One of these considerations, and it now lay at the front of his thoughts, was that he had put Bess on the office payroll in 1941 and by 1944 she was drawing $4,500 a year, a handsome salary in those days, the top salary among his office staff. As if this were not bad enough, he had put his sister, Mary Jane, on the payroll beginning September 1, 1943, at $1,800 a year.

The payroll padding was a poor idea; it does not accord with Truman's historical image as a man honest in all his dealings, and there was no excuse for it, save that he had given in, collapsed, before a pressure that had beset him for years. It was a pressure that has no easy explanation. The present pages are not the place to relate Truman's financial problems, but suffice to say that when he was a farmer in Jackson County, Missouri, from 1906 until 1917, he worked a big and prosperous farm; in the 1920s and early 1930s as a county executive he made a good salary, and in the Senate he received

$10,000 a year, a princely sum. He supported relatives, on his own side, his mother and sister, and on his wife's side, her mother. In the depths of the depression he might have supported his brother, Vivian, and two of Bess's brothers, all married with children. He obtained a Federal Housing Administration job for Vivian, and gave county architectural fees to Fred Wallace and got George Wallace into the county highway department. But his Wallace brothers-in-law liked to drink, and they may have drunk up their incomes and more. His wife was sensitive to their troubles and possibly gave them money. She may not have been much of a manager with her own household. Truman doubtless hesitated to criticize her.

The moral issue of putting Bess and Mary Jane on the payroll does not seem to have concerned him. Other senators did it, or gave speeches for which they took fees.[43]

His only concern in 1944 was that if he accepted the vice-presidential nomination reporters would write background stories, and what would he say to his wife when they spread her name over their newspapers?

The payroll problem moved him to call his closest personal friend in Kansas City, a tall, gangly owner of a chain of drugstores, Tom L. Evans, who had supported him politically through thick and thin. Evans would do anything for him.

The conversation was short and to the point. "Are you my friend?" he asked.

"I hope so, why?" was the response.

"If you are, I need you up here to help keep me from being Vice President. How soon can you get up?"

"I can come right away."

"Well, come on I need you."

Not knowing the reason for all this, Evans was incredulous. "Don't kid me," he said, "anybody wants to be Vice President if he can. You know who I am; don't kid me."

When he arrived it was to learn that Truman had "skeletons" in his closet. "Well, now wait a minute," he contended. "This is something I don't know anything about. I didn't know you had skeletons. What are they? Maybe I wouldn't want you to run neither, but you've got to tell me what are these skeletons?"

"Well," was the abject response, "the worst thing is that I've had the boss," meaning Mrs. Truman, "on the payroll in my Senate office and I'm not going to have her name drug over the front pages of the paper and over the radio."

"Well, lord," said Tom, "that isn't anything too great." After a while he talked him out of it.

In any event, not much came of the payroll problem. When Bess's payroll presence became known shortly after the convention, on July 26, Clare Boothe Luce, wife of the publisher of *Time* and *Life* and running for reelection as a Republican congresswoman in Connecticut, described Mrs. Truman as "Payroll Bess"; the senator's office in turn put out a release describing how his wife came regularly to the office and worked there: "Mrs. Truman handles all the Senator's personal mail and works on the editing of the Committee Reports. She comes into the office two or three times a week and takes the material home with her. She works with the Senator on it at night, since he has no time for it during office hours." This was not true, but the release said it was. In 1942 the senator, momentarily in Durham, North Carolina, wrote his wife, "I'm sure glad you went to the office. It's much better for you to go there a few days a week and see what goes on. . . . You don't have to say a word only just drop in and do some signing. It helps all concerned."

Presumably the other skeleton was having Mary Jane on the payroll. It does not appear to have come up, although it should have. Mary Jane could not have worked in the senator's office because she lived in Grandview, Missouri, and spent all her time caring for the senator's aged mother, Mrs. Martha Ellen Truman. She had never been to Washington, and she visited it only after her brother became president.

Bess and Mary Jane remained on the payroll during the 1944 campaign, and when Truman became vice-president they went on his vice-presidential payroll, where they remained until he became president.[44]

When Tom Evans was learning about skeletons in Chicago in July 1944, he heard Truman say he could not afford another campaign. He had borrowed money for both Senate campaigns in 1940 from a life insurance policy. Evans dismissed this problem; the national committee would take care of the vice-presidential campaign.[45] One wonders why Truman raised the issue—was it an effort to justify what he had done with the payroll?

In her recent biography of her mother, Margaret Truman advanced still another reason her father did not want the nomination. This was something Margaret discovered that summer when one of her Wallace aunts told her that her grandfather, her mother's father, David W. Wallace, had committed suicide in 1903. In those days, even as late as the 1940s, suicides were family disgraces, and Margaret believes David Wallace's suicide bothered her father very much when he was considering the vice-presidency. It would become public knowledge. Bess Truman had never told her daughter about this family matter. And how to deal with her aged mother, Mrs. Wallace, then living with the Trumans in Washington?[46]

Margaret's biography of her mother is an attractive book and contains many shrewd insights. No student of her father's rise to the presidency can ignore what she has written about her mother and, necessarily, her mother's relation to her father's career. But the suicide issue is unbelievable. Would Truman's wife, married back in a time when wives announced they would love, honor, and obey, have refused her husband the vice-presidency, which meant the presidency? Could not Mrs. Wallace, a sweet, careful old lady, who had made a career out of remembering the way in which her husband died, have put her feelings aside, just once?

There was one last consideration that must have bothered Truman as he thought over what lay before him. That was the feeling his wife held against the presidency itself. Where she got it is hard to say. It may have had some association with the Roosevelts. Perhaps because of what happened in 1940, Bess Truman never seems to have thought much of Roosevelt. She and her husband abhorred the publicity that surrounded Eleanor Roosevelt, not understanding how an empty marriage pushed the president's wife into a public career. The Trumans privately deplored the divorces of the Roosevelt children. Bess's dislike of the White House may also have had something to do with her husband's feelings about the newspaper press; Truman believed reporters were decent people, but their publishers would do anything for the sheer joy of wrecking some innocent person's reputation, especially that of a political leader. Somehow she developed a hatred of the notion that her husband might achieve the presidency. She put the possibility out of mind as long as she could. When things heated up during the convention she was in what can only be described as a bad frame of mind; it was necessary for her and her daughter to attend convention sessions, and as events came closer to the nomination Mrs. Truman's face hardened into an irritability that photographers easily captured. She relaxed into smiles and grins during the convention's ultimate moments, wearing her "Truman for V.P." ribbon and doing what was necessary. When it was all over she said the right things, though she slipped at first, saying she was "reconciled" to the nomination, but then said that "this morning I'm beginning to like it." Margaret wrote years later that when the shouting was over and the Trumans drove back to Independence her mother did not say a word and the temperature in the car was close to arctic.[47]

To return to the candidacy. A presidential notification was necessary, as Truman told Hannegan months earlier when the commissioner of internal revenue was asked by the president to become national chairman—the senator told Hannegan to wait until the president asked him personally. The party leaders, too, wanted Truman thus notified, for time was running out. Byrnes announced his withdrawal Wednesday morning at 11:15 with release of a letter to Senator Burnet Maybank of South Carolina, "in deference to the wishes of the president," a formula, so he wrote later, designed for the occasion. It was necessary to get Truman's candidacy, widely bruited, into the open. The leaders called the president late that afternoon—lunchtime on the West Coast—and arranged to have the candidate in Hannegan's suite when they put through the call. Present were Walker, Flynn, Kelly, Allen, and Boss Frank Hague of Jersey City. Truman sat on one twin bed, Hannegan on the other. As Roosevelt spoke, Hannegan held out the receiver. The president always talked in such a loud voice that it was necessary to get the receiver away from one's ear. Roosevelt's well-known voice filled the room. He asked if Hannegan had gotten "that fellow" lined up. The chairman said no, he was acting like a damned Missouri mule.

"Well," came the response, "tell him if he wants to break up the Democratic Party in the middle of a war that's his responsibility." With that, the president banged down the receiver.

"Now what do you say?" asked Hannegan.

As Truman remembered, he said, "Jesus Christ!"[48]

He may have added, "Why the hell didn't he tell me in the first place?"

He had no idea that the president and Hannegan had orchestrated the call, having agreed beforehand what each one would say.[49]

But all that was beside the point: he had the confirmation he needed.

Afterward he went around to see Byrnes, to say he had not been working behind Byrnes's back. Byrnes of course knew that, as he had been working behind Truman's back all along.

— 3 —

ROOSEVELT AND TRUMAN!

The final drama in the choice of Harry S. Truman took place in the Chicago Stadium, as it was called. It was a big barn of a hall near the center of the city that could seat twenty-four thousand people, and if they stood up in aisles and balconies it would hold maybe ten thousand more. To this mecca came the Democratic party faithful in mid-July 1944 to yell, shout, vote, whatever would bring victory in the November election.

Democrats converged upon Chicago from all over the country. The group from New York City was perhaps a bit special, in credentials as well as size. A reporter from the *New York Times* interviewed its most prominent member, the former national chairman, Farley, as he boarded the Twentieth Century Limited. Farley refused to say much—he had given up the state chairmanship some weeks before and was only a delegate at large. Another traveler to Chicago was the secretary of Tammany Hall, Bert Stand, who left by plane from La Guardia Field. He made up for some of Farley's silences. Asked who he would back he said it would be "Roosevelt on the first ballot and Roosevelt on all ballots." He refused to commit himself on the vice-presidency, merely saying, "Whoever Mr. Roosevelt wants, we will back." Asked about the role of Farley, who had become an executive for the Coca-Cola Company, he said he thought Farley would be "pretty busy selling Coca-Cola." "If he sees this," said Stand, "he will thank me for the plug."[1]

A few delegates, like the Tammany secretary, traveled by plane, but only a few: it was difficult to gain access to the strictly rationed seats. Most arrived by train. Wartime trains, to be sure, were a difficult means of travel. They were crowded with servicemen and harried civilian travelers. Pullmans and compartments were available only for people who reserved long ahead of time; all others crowded aboard and sat in coaches not much changed from the time of William McKinley and the Republican Roosevelt. At night weary passengers tried to sleep, difficult in the heat of midsummer with no air-conditioning. Conductors turned on lights at every station stop. In daytime passengers looked out dirty windows at nearly interminable open spaces as mile after mile of middle western or western or southern landscape glided by. All this accompanied by the clickety-clack of unwelded rails.

Over the weekend of July 15–16 delegates staggered in. The lobby of the huge Stevens, later known as the Hilton, filled with talkers, sometimes picturesquely garbed westerners or southerners, together with all sorts of hangers-on who wanted to see what was happening. Delegates walked around wearing their badges; all were decked with emblems of states and régions, proud to show off, even more proud to be present at their party's great quadrennial assemblage.

Chicago Stadium, meanwhile, was getting its decorations. Thirty-eight cardboard cutouts, life-sized and highly colored, of servicemen and service women in grim battle poses, charged toward delegates' seats from every corner of the hall. Red-white-and-blue fluorescent victory Vs were arranged to light up when the stadium darkened after the playing of the national anthem. Over the balcony, in imposing rows, were affixed greatly enlarged black-and-white likenesses of the country's fourteen Democratic presidents, from Thomas Jefferson to FDR. An eight-foot colored image of Roosevelt's face looked down on the convention floor from the highest point in the northwest girders. "Same one we used four years ago," said the superintendent of the Chicago Sewer Bureau, Tom Garry, who was in charge. "Retouched," he explained. "It was a little pale."[2]

J. G. Grouzard, in charge of concessions, was getting ready for the crowds. He was clearly disappointed in the appetites and thirsts of the Republicans who had used the stadium for their convention just a few weeks earlier. He had overestimated the hunger of the Republicans and arranged for 50,000 hot dogs, but the Republicans ate only 30,000. Based on the Republicans' appetites, for the Democrats he prepared only 30,000 hot dogs; however, at Thursday's session delegates and visitors ate 25,000 hot dogs, and the next day almost as many. By convention's end they had doubled or better the sandwich figures of all previous conventions. As for drinks, Grouzard prepared 125,000 soft-drink items and 96,000 bottles of beer. Excluding Wednesday, opening day, on Thursday and Friday the Democrats drank 125,000 bottles of pop and 80,000 bottles of beer. Democratic consumption of hard liquor surpassed—tripled—anything recorded at previous national conventions of either major party: 300 quarts of bourbon, rye, and scotch.

During the days before the convention the delegates rested up, as they needed to do after their travels, but, alas, displayed a few irritabilities. Democrats, like Republicans, could dislike each other; it was asking too much to think that delegates from everywhere in the country would exude nothing but nice thoughts about each other. Argument even broke out within state delegations. In the case of the California delegation—California, where the heat of the sun beat hard upon hatless individuals, possibly twisting their thoughts— weak party allegiances, devotion of some delegates to Wallace, and a feud between adherents of former governor Culbert L. Olson and Attorney General Robert W. Kenny caused party division. Olson and Kenny, both delegates, could not tolerate each other. Before the delegation left its home state Olson undertook to denounce Kenny as a source of dissension in the state party. Kenny retorted, "You have just heard the swan song of a lame duck." Olson later told an interviewer he thought at the time, "I would rather be a dead duck than a live snake." To this pleasantry Kenny responded, "This piece of herpetology undoubtedly was an afterthought." The Kenny-Olson feud, in full view at the convention, became known as a phase of California's political zoology.[3]

Perhaps because of the feud, the California delegates were unable to concentrate on the fact that in their midst was the first Chinese American ever elected a delegate to a national convention. Some had represented Hawaii, but it was not yet a state. The man was Albert K. Chow, a notary public from Chinatown in San Francisco.

The former actress Helen Douglas, wife of actor Melvyn Douglas, added pulchritude to the California group, and also something of a sharp tongue. Her husband was in the military, and she was doing her part by running for Congress. At the convention she told a press conference that the Republicans at their Chicago convention had given too much attention to her GOP opposite, Congresswoman Luce. They had made Mrs. Douglas's life difficult. "I have great respect for

Mrs. Luce," she said. "I'm not a fencer. I'm not a wit. I don't say things smarter than other people."[4]

Present also were the dozen southern delegations, several of which arrived in a state of unhappiness verging on rebellion. Unlike the Californians, their rancors were not so personal. They unfortunately possessed no spokespersons, to use the later word, who, like Helen Douglas, could introduce a little repartee. Here the Texas delegation was in the worst shape, for internecine fighting had resulted in a delegation that was voting forty-five to three against Roosevelt. Because of Texas alone, it was clear the president could not be nominated unanimously; the Texans would throw their votes to Senator Byrd. It was said Byrd might obtain between 150 and 200 votes in the convention total of 1,170. A rump, pro-Roosevelt delegation had come up from Texas, and its members were imploring the credentials committee to seat them rather than their opponents. The convention split the delegation's votes, giving half to the rump group, and thirty-three members of the regular delegation walked out. The South Carolina delegation also was opposed by a rump delegation, all black, which would not obtain recognition.

Behind southern dissension lay anti-Roosevelt feeling, and behind that lay racism: many southerners felt that the president had thrust Wallace, a liberal, on the convention in 1940 and was himself weakening on the racial issue. The convention's conservatives, including virtually all southerners, wanted to reaffirm the racial plank of 1940: "We pledge to uphold due process and the equal protection of the laws for every citizen, regardless of race, creed or color." Northern Negroes were unwilling to go along with that, and indeed could not, as the Republicans already had adopted a much stronger plank. The race issue would "snarl" the platform, wrote a reporter, with a certain forgetfulness of metaphor.[5] On that issue the CIO leader Murray foresaw a terrible state of affairs if the snarl did not get straightened: "God help America if, after this War is won overseas, we should find ourselves plunged here at home into a terrifying war of hatred because of intolerance, race, religion or color. I plead on behalf of my organization for the inclusion of a plank on this vital issue, a plank that people will understand. They want to know that the Democratic party has taken a courageous stand on this all important issue."

The convention on Thursday, July 20, at last outdid the GOP, adopting a strong plank, many southerners shouting nay. That was all they could do, for it was necessary to get twelve states, the full South, to bring the issue to the floor, and several southern states were dragging their feet.[6]

As an outlet for southern dissatisfaction the regular Texas delegates were soliciting, with considerable success, Byrd votes among delegates from Florida, Mississippi, Louisiana, and Virginia. The danger was that they could get more. Wallace could not keep them from doing it. Only one southern state was pledged to go down the line for a Roosevelt-Wallace ticket and that was Georgia, its delegation loyal to Governor Ellis G. Arnall. Part of the Florida delegation favored Wallace. Otherwise Wallace had not a single pledged vote in the entire South.

It was ironic that as the Republicans encountered no trouble on the race issue and had a great deal of trouble drawing up a foreign policy plank, for the Democrats it was vice versa (the Democratic foreign policy plank went right down the line for everything President Roosevelt had said and done and passed with no argument).

A much smaller issue among the delegations was adoption of a plank favoring the equal rights amendment to the Constitution. The amendment had originated in 1923. The Republicans were advocating it, and Emma Guffey Miller, sister of Senator Joe Guffey, appeared in Chicago before the resolutions subcommittee and advocated it. Among opponents were Marvin Harrison of Cleveland, representative of the National Consumers League, who described it as "this lunatic proposal." Also against was the National Catholic Welfare Council, the National League of Women Voters, the National Board of the YWCA, and the American Association of University Women. Murray was against it, as was Secretary of Labor Frances Perkins; both testified in Chicago on Monday. On Thursday, the convention's second day, when the issue went to the floor, the delegates came out in favor.[7]

Women generally received attention in Chicago. Chairman Hannegan told the convention that with many men absent in the armed forces the support of women was essential. On the first night Gladys Tillett of North Carolina, assistant chairwoman, made the same point in an address ("As you know, the Democratic fortunes will be in large part due to the votes of women"). As convention secretary, Dorothy Vredenburgh of Alabama kept the issue before the delegates when voting began—she announced the roll call of states. Women delegates received instruction in political techniques, attending school at the Stevens on the morning of Wednesday, July 19. Hannegan was the instructor, followed by others. The overflow audience listened and took notes. Teachers described press releases, radio programs, and how to address street crowds from stepladders. They assigned homework and scheduled another session for Friday, July 21.

At last the moment came: on Wednesday, at 12:04 P.M., the national chairman called the convention to order. The secretary read the "Call for Convention," followed by welcoming addresses by Mayor Kelly and Senator Lucas. Hannegan introduced Kelly as a great American, a great mayor of a great city. When the mayor mentioned the name of the greatest American of all, delegates rose and cheered, with the exception of the Texas delegation and scattered malcontents. Initial business at end, all present listened to Pauley give the financial report, which informed them how poor the party was, its surplus funds "very, very small."[8]

The big event of the first day was the keynote address that evening. After dinner the crowd drifted in, gradually filling the topmost seats in the hall. As people were entering, the rump Texas delegates made an impromptu march, carrying banners announcing, "We Want Roosevelt," "Help Us Clean House in Texas," and "Throw the Judases Out." When Vice-President Wallace entered to take his seat in the Iowa delegation an informal demonstration broke out, lasting several minutes, accompanied by whistles, cheers, and applause. Through the hall many standards waved enthusiastically. At 9:05 the evening session opened, and Hannegan introduced Gladys Tillett. When she finished at 10:47, the chairman read a news bulletin announcing that the Hideki Tōjō cabinet in Tokyo had resigned; delegates greeted the news with wild cheering. (What they did not know, and no American could have known, was that in faraway East Prussia the German underground was about to place a bomb in a briefcase under a table in Adolf Hitler's command bunker, very nearly killing Germany's leader. Failure of the assassination attempt of July 20 was to bring a terrible vengeance upon the conspirators and condemn Europe to ten more months of slaughter by the opposing armies.)

Then came the keynoter, Governor Robert S. Kerr of Oklahoma. For a short time, reported Turner Catledge, rancors among delegates softened and almost disappeared in the stream of Kerr's oratory. A big, broad-shouldered man, accustomed to prairie audiences, Kerr shouted his speech, which everyone could have heard without the microphones; he must have reminded older auditors of William Jennings Bryan, whose booming voice reached three city blocks, and who became a "peerless orator" for that reason until introduction of "loudspeakers" at the national conventions in 1920.

The speech itself was good old-fashioned spellbinding. Kerr opened by denouncing the administration of former president Herbert Hoover (who in 1944 was hale and hearty and must have winced if he listened over the radio). The Republicans, the orator shouted, had placed the mantle of Hoover on the shoulders of his cherished disciple, Thomas E. Dewey. But it was no mantle, it was a shroud! From that moment the audience was with Kerr, and he could draw applause whenever he wanted. He drew the greatest for the high point of his speech, an argument against youth, personified by Dewey, in favor of age and experience. What would Churchill and Stalin think, he asked, when they learned that Dewey looked on them as just tired old men? Were admirals Chester W. Nimitz, William F. (Bull) Halsey, and Ernest J. King, or General Douglas MacArthur, tired old men? Nimitz, the youngest, was fifty-seven, MacArthur sixty-four, King sixty-six.

Who could think of discarding American leaders or "the 62-year-old Roosevelt as their commander in chief"? At that pronouncement a parade started before the speakers' stand, and Kerr donned a ten-gallon white hat to review it. He reached for the standards of the Philippine Islands and Hawaii and waved them. The Texas delegation was standing but did not wave their banners in return, and people tried to tear the banners away from them. The standards of Tennessee, Virginia, and Mississippi were rigid. Connecticut delegates paraded their standard with a sign affixed, "We Want Wallace!"

After about twenty minutes Kerr shouted into the microphones, "I've got some other questions I want to ask Mr. Dewey!" He looked up and grinned and added, "Is it all right if I ask them?" The delegates settled slowly into their places, and he finished at 11:57 P.M.[9]

The next day the *New York Times* published an editorial asking for something less prejudicial to the judgment of the independent voter than Kerr's speech, perhaps a combination of a calliope and a cannon. Kerr, it said, beheld not a single virtue in American life "not the achievement of the party led by Mr. Roosevelt." There was not a single misfortune "for which the party led by Mr. Dewey is not responsible."[10]

Kerr's oratory, it turned out, performed miracles only for the moment, and it could not permanently calm all the irritabilities the delegates brought with them. After the evening session delegates forgot most of what Kerr told them, and the next morning were busily embroidering their differences.

Prior to nominations and choice of a vice-presidential candidate, the convention's time was taken up by nomination of the president for his fourth term. Here, behind the scenes, difficulty appeared over whether Senator Barkley would make the nominating speech, as he had promised the president he would do. The question arose when Walker, leaving a dinner given by Mayor Kelly on Wednesday evening and after the telephone call to Roosevelt concerning Truman, saw Barkley at a table in the Blackstone dining room. Because he and the senator had been friendly he felt it was the right thing to do to tell him of the choice of Truman. He phrased the news as best he could: "I felt the nice thing to do was to tell him that President Roosevelt had asked a group of us to support Truman for vice-president." Barkley was dumbstruck. He was very much put out and indicated he did not know if he would nominate the president. Several times that night Les Biffle came to Walker's room relating that he was having great trouble convincing Barkley to go ahead. Finally, at about three or four o'clock in the morning, he came in and said Barkley would speak but was still going to submit his name to the convention. That Thursday, Walker noticed Barkley's son-in-law talking with a mutual friend, both doing their utmost to advance the senator's candidacy.[11]

Fortunately not much of Barkley's ill humor became known, at the time or even later. The mayor of Louisville, Wilson Wyatt, went to see the senator during this troubled time and heard the former national chairman, Farley, say, recalling what the president had done to Farley's vice-presidential aspirations in 1940, "Alben, you have been double-crossed by the boss—just as I was." In his memoirs a decade later Barkley toned down the conversation. He had a number of "conferences" with the former chairman, he admitted, "but I do not recall any action or statement on my part that should have led him to feel I was about to tear up my speech."[12] In his memoirs he did recall talking to Byrnes at this time and thoughtfully attributed his own sentiments to the former assistant president. For two hours, he wrote, he and Byrnes "licked each other's sores with heartfelt sympathy." Then Byrnes said, "You are going to nominate Roosevelt, aren't you?"

"Yes," Barkley answered.

"If I were you," said Byrnes, "I wouldn't say anything too complimentary about him."

The senator responded with a query, "I can't nominate a man without complimenting him, how can I do that?"

In preparation for his memoirs Barkley taped a massive series of conversations with the writer Sidney Shalett, and the tapes added to the above conversation, again quoting Byrnes: "I wouldn't be very enthusiastic about it," he repeated. "I'd just do it in a very formal, casual way, do your duty."[13]

As Barkley amended the historical record, omitting his own thoughts and quoting Byrnes's in extenso—Byrnes by then was out of national politics, rusticating in South Carolina, and Barkley was back in the Senate—so later did Byrnes rearrange a few things. He, however, was much more diplomatic. His book came out four years after Barkley's. By that time the Kentucky senator had passed to his heavenly reward, appropriately in the middle of a rousing speech at Washington and Lee University. Byrnes could have written of Barkley's discomfiture at the hands of the president. He did nothing of the sort. As for his own discomfiture, he did what the Kansas journalist William Allen White once said President McKinley did to him after an impertinent question: he crawled up on a pedestal and turned to marble. "I freely admit I was disappointed, and felt hurt by President Roosevelt's action," he concluded. "Not having wanted to be involved, I was angry with myself for permitting the President to get me in it. But I cherished no animosity toward him."[14]

At the Chicago convention the president's nomination went off with éclat, whatever the preliminaries. Barkley intoned that Roosevelt was endowed with "the intellectual boldness of Thomas Jefferson, the indomitable courage of Andrew Jackson, the faith and patience of Abraham Lincoln, the rugged integrity of Grover Cleveland, and the scholarly vision of Woodrow Wilson." When at last, having held back in the expected way, he mentioned the president's name, twenty thousand people leaped to their feet. It was pandemonium, what with shrill screams from women, hoarse shouts from men, "the organ's thunder, the blaring bands in the galleries, the din of hand-wound sirens," all beating "in ringing waves against all eardrums." Paraders sang, zigged, pirouetted, cavorted, "cut capers simply, in pairs and—where there was space—in ring-around-rosie groups." Delegates and observers frantically turned newspapers, pamphlets, and programs into confetti and dropped it from balconies or threw it in the air from the floor, where it fell like silver snow, turning and twisting in the blue-white brilliance of the klieg lights and covering the heads and shoulders of marchers. Everywhere blinked the flash-lights of photographers. At last the convention's permanent chair-man, Senator Jackson, called the assemblage to order.[15]

After the seconding speeches the balloting showed the inevitable: only ninety votes were in opposition, of which eighty-nine were for Byrd and one for Farley. Two Farley friends in the New York delega-tion each cast a half ballot, with Farley casting his half ballot for Byrd. Except those one and one-half votes against Roosevelt, all the others were from the South.

In the balloting Florida's spokesman introduced some welcome levity. Rattled, he announced: "Fourteen votes for Mr. Roosevelt, four birds for Mr. Byrd."[16]

From San Diego that evening, the president accepted the nomina-tion in a speech that was attractively short, just a few minutes. To hear the familiar voice disembodied was a strange experience, al-though he had spoken by radio to the Chicago convention in 1940 and similarly to the Philadelphia convention in 1936. He opened his reelection bid on the note of "experience" versus "immaturity." He said he was too busy, the war emergency too serious, to permit him to engage in an active campaign.

Byrnes was not there for the president's speech, by that time having left for Washington. During the seconding speeches he sat on the platform, and he and Hannegan talked. The national chairman told of the conversation the day before with the president and Roose-velt's request that Truman be nominated. He said the president was much concerned as to what Byrnes was saying and how he was taking the decision against him. Hannegan asked Byrnes to talk to the president when he got in touch with him again that evening. Byrnes told Hannegan to tell the president that because he was a "political liability" it would be foolish for him to give Roosevelt political advice.[17]

1

Wallace's supreme effort to obtain the nomination took place on Thursday evening after the president's speech. It was an extraordinary venture that seemed to come close to victory. In a well-known, classic procedure, the Wallace people tried to stampede the convention.

Looking to the annals of history there was no real reason why the Wallace supporters needed to fail. Indeed, stampedes had been a notable, respectable part of American politics over the preceding half century. The young Bryan had tried it in 1896 and done it in a single speech, the famous address about the gold standard ("You shall not crucify mankind upon a cross of gold"). He was thirty-six, a former one-term congressman from Nebraska, without support from the conservative Cleveland side of the party, but when he spread his arms in the form of a cross after his famous line, the crowd turned into a shouting mob. In the annals of conventions the Republicans actually had done more stampeding than the Democrats. Their convention of 1920 under control of a senatorial clique gave the presidential nomination to Senator Warren G. Harding of Ohio, after two much more prominent candidates, Major General Leonard Wood and Governor Frank O. Lowden of Illinois, fought each other to a standstill. The clique was all ready to nominate Senator Irvine L. Lenroot of Wisconsin for the vice-presidency when a small, haggard delegate from Oregon, Wallace McCamant, stood on a chair and shouted for "a man who is sterling in his Americanism and stands for all that the Republican Party holds dear," Governor Calvin Coolidge of Massachusetts, raising an uproar and thereby choosing the president when Harding died in 1923. Twenty years later, in 1940, the Republicans stampeded again, this time to the little-known New York utilities lawyer Willkie.[18]

Reviewing the history of stampedes, Attorney General Francis

Biddle afterward made an interesting observation about Wallace's bid for the vice-presidential nomination in 1944 that appeared to carry a considerable truth. Bryan and Willkie, he remarked, were unknown figures; Wallace was too well known. He said nothing about Coolidge, who had a national reputation in 1920 and thus ruined his theory.[19]

Wallace did not fail for want of trying. It is probable that during his journey to Mongolia, China, and Siberia, just prior to the convention, he mapped out his strategy. He must have noticed the president's dallying with other candidates, a strange procedure for a running mate who insisted upon him in 1940. Too, what happened at the Chicago convention simply could not have been done without planning. Wallace must have laid his plans while abroad and then, after his first disquieting meeting with Roosevelt on Monday, July 10, put them to the test.

The Wallace plan to overwhelm the convention with a stampede had its worst moment with release of the president's letter to Jackson, which occurred on Monday evening, July 17. Hannegan, the day before, having momentarily gone over to Byrnes, began to put the heat on Wallace's supporters, announcing the letter's existence and approximate contents, thus producing an atmosphere of uncertainty. He prophesied that the letter would be delivered into Jackson's hands the next day, Monday, else Tuesday. Speaking to a hundred reporters he found himself under a veritable barrage, but he would say only that the letter would speak for itself, and that while he knew its contents it was only in a general way.

When Jackson released the letter the convention's conservatives immediately beheld no clear-cut endorsement, and in fact read it as the opposite. Byrnes supporters (and soon thereafter those of Truman) described it as a "kiss of death." Farley, who was supporting neither side but was an avowed conservative, wrote afterward, "If there ever was a left-handed endorsement, that was it." Asked by Warren Moscow of the *New York Times,* Senator Elmer Thomas of Oklahoma essayed, "It will tend to defeat the man it was intended to help."[20]

Senator Truman carefully put himself in the middle, which was where he had been in terms of the nomination until almost that precise moment, venturing, "Naturally I expect the president to stick to his friends."[21]

Wallace supporters gradually regained their composure and announced the letter as something for which to be grateful. Senator James M. Tunnell of Delaware avowed, "It's a great letter." Wallace's leading Senate champion, Guffey, said it was a good letter and predicted renomination. Helen Douglas, always an enthusiast, stood above the debate. She was good to have around. She asked for a closing of ranks in the California delegation and ideally all delegations. "Let's not talk about anybody but Mr. Wallace," she said. "The California delegation just has to support him—California is for him wholeheartedly. If we didn't vote for him we just couldn't go back to California—we'd have to go to some other state."[22]

Shortly after release of the letter Wallace's stock rose because of a reason quite apart from the Roosevelt endorsement. The Wallace people realized that if on Monday evening they had not received the world's greatest letter, their opponents nonetheless were in disarray. Rumor circulated that Byrnes would withdraw, a rumor that became fact on Wednesday morning. Truman supporters were trying to organize but found themselves dealing with a candidate whose mulish qualities were not tamed until Wednesday afternoon. Guffey took heart. "When I first entered politics," he announced, "my father told me to remember one thing, 'You can't beat somebody with nobody.'"[23] For that short two-day period Wallace had no serious competition. Barkley wanted the nomination but the possibility, he knew inwardly, was unlikely. Several state delegations had decided to endorse favorite sons, such as North Carolina's governor J. Melville Broughton. The *New York Times* reporter Hagerty asked Josephus Daniels about Broughton and the elder Daniels (father of Jonathan, newspaper editor, the president's superior as Secretary of the Navy during the Wilson administration) averred that the governor could go on the stump and carry the banner. Asked what he thought of Wallace he said he thought highly of him but was glad the party had many other well-qualified individuals.[24]

The confusion came to an end Wednesday afternoon, but that was the day Wallace arrived in Chicago. What could the conservatives do, even if they managed to unite behind Truman? The vice-president of the United States was in fighting trim, in what he described as a fight to the finish. He left the Washington train at the Sixty-third Street station to avoid the crowd of reporters he knew would be at the terminal. The train was two hours late. When he reached his hotel, the Sherman, he nonetheless found two thousand people cheering him. As he entered the hotel a group of college students greeted him and marched through the lobby singing a Wallace song to the tune of "Joshua Fit the Battle of Jericho":

> You can talk about Senator Barkley.
> You can talk about Jimmy Byrnes.
> You can talk about Senator Truman.
> But the Democratic party has learned that
> Wallace fought the battle for the common man,
> Common man, common man.
> Wallace fought the battle for the common man.
> And he'll fight that battle again.

To a crowded room full of reporters and friends he said he had not decided to come until the day before, Tuesday. "Did the letter from President Roosevelt to Senator Jackson meet your wishes?" He said it did. "Did the President throw you down or endorse you?" He did exactly, said the vice-president, as Wallace had asked. Reporters asked if he had seen Hillman, and he refused to reply, ending the conference. Thereafter he went to his headquarters on the mezzanine floor, thence to the suite of the Iowa state chairman, Jake More, where he saw Kenny of California, Helen Douglas, Senator Pepper of Florida, Senator Guffey, and Governor Arnall. He later had a conference with Hillman and Murray at the Morrison Hotel.[25]

By Wednesday afternoon Truman supporters were beginning to move, sometimes successfully, sometimes barely holding their own. Reports were coming from the New York state delegation, which possessed ninety-six votes, that Truman was the choice of the anti-Wallace forces. Earlier, it was stated, Flynn, in a conference with New York state leaders, informed them that the decision of the Wallace opponents was to back Truman, and that the New York delegation might vote for him after the first ballot. Truman had told the Missouri delegation he did not want the vice-presidency, this in his role as chairman of the delegation, but someone arranged for him to be called to the door of the room, and before he could stop his friends the entire delegation voted to put him forward. In the Pennsylvania delegation the Wallace-ites proposed to instruct the group to vote as a unit. Walker asked the state chairman, Mayor David Lawrence of

Pittsburgh, if the vote would bind those present, in which case, Walker said, he wanted to absent himself. He was much embarrassed to have to say this, as Murray was sitting behind him and glowering. Lawrence said the vote was not binding, and Walker was pleased to see that in a mostly pro-Wallace delegation—the vote was forty-four to twenty-one—the mayor, understanding the situation, voted with him against the Wallace supporters.[26]

Everything came down to Thursday, when Roosevelt was nominated. When Wallace appeared before the convention to second the nomination of Roosevelt, he received an ovation.

An incident took place just before Wallace's seconding speech that astonished Pauley, who was sharing with Hannegan a little office directly under the speaker's platform. It was, he thought later, the strangest incident of the whole convention. He was talking on the telephone to the president aboard his private train, giving the latest news and setting out in detail the progress of the plan to thwart Wallace's renomination, when he looked up and saw himself staring "at the one man with whom I was most unlikely to discuss such things." Wallace had walked into his office, awaiting his turn on the speakers' stand.

He stood there, Pauley remembered vividly, "briefcase in hand, looking at me." His campaign manager was with him, and Pauley could do nothing other than end his conversation with the president. "There was a sticky, sweating silence in that close little office and then I said, 'Well, at least you've heard it play-by-play.'"

Wallace did not speak for a moment. Ignoring the telephone call he finally said, "This is my campaign speech," tapping his briefcase, "this is the one that will do it."

The nonplussed Pauley said Wallace pulled out his speech, left his briefcase in the office, went up on the stand, "and made what was, in his opinion, the most inspiring talk he had ever given."[27]

The name Roosevelt is revered in the remotest corners in this earth. The name Roosevelt is cursed only by Germans, Japs, and certain American troglodytes. . . . The voice of our New World liberals must carry on. . . . We must finish this job before the Nation can breathe in safety. The boys at the front know this better than anyone else. . . . Roosevelt is a greater liberal today than he has ever been. His soul is pure. . . . He thinks big. He sees far. There is no question about the

renomination of President Roosevelt by this convention. The only question is whether the convention and the party workers believe wholeheartedly in the liberal policies for which Roosevelt has always stood.[28]

That night, just before the president spoke to the convention,
the Wallace-ites, undetected, packed the convention hall, readying
themselves for the stampede. The party leaders may have taken too
much comfort in the arrangements Mayor Kelly had made to avoid
any group's taking over the galleries or getting unauthorized supporters onto the floor. Ticket takers and ushers apparently were
Chicago policemen in mufti and completely under Kelly's control.
His henchmen had produced books of tickets for authorized persons,
and the tickets looked like dollar bills and would have been nearly
impossible to counterfeit. Each ticket related the day and session for
which it was valid. But the single error he made was enough to ruin
everything: all tickets were printed in the same color. For the Thursday night session, the stampede, Wallace supporters seem to have
used every ticket in every book they had, knowing that in the rush at
the gates the takers and ushers would not have time to check the
tickets for the proper day and session.[29]

Gaining entrance both to galleries and floor, Wallace supporters in
the thousands packed the stadium to the highest seats under the eaves.
The hall resembled a Wallace rally rather than a convention, backers
spreading banners through galleries and floor, displaying such slogans
as "We Want Wallace," "Keep the Winning Team, Roosevelt and Wallace," and "The People Want Wallace." Truman banners appeared,
reading, "Truman for Vice President," first among Missouri delegates,
then elsewhere, but Wallace banners were everywhere.

The convention opened its fourth session at 9:04 P.M., with Helen
Douglas as first speaker, then the war correspondent Quentin Reynolds. By 10:00, in the midst of Reynolds's speech, floor aisles were so
crowded it was almost impossible for anyone to push through. No one
was sure where the people came from, but police said no such crowd
had ever jammed the stadium, even in prior political conventions. Reynolds ended at 10:15 and received an ovation. Jackson asked for silence
while the president spoke over the radio. The president ended at 10:35.
The crowd cheered, and after three minutes Jackson cut them off with
"The Star-Spangled Banner."

Then arose the dangerous moment. "We want Wallace!" was the chant. The convention organist, Al Melgard, perhaps paid by someone, maybe in ignorance, took up the theme, playing the Iowa state song, "Iowa, Iowa, that's where the tall corn grows!" Floor and galleries bloomed with Roosevelt-Wallace banners. Wallace parades began.

How to handle the melee—the stampede? The party leaders were furious: who was running the convention, anyway? Pauley described the demonstrators as "a strange mixture of actual Communists, would-be Communists, do-gooders and other hypertension personalities who had jumped on his [Wallace's] bandwagon, ruthlessly shoving aside a small core of men and women who sincerely believed Henry Wallace was the only answer to a troubled world. With such a lunatic fringe the Wallace forces were emotionally organized to commit anything up to and including hari-kari."[30]

Such may not have been true, but to the leaders the Wallace enthusiasts were completely out of order, defying the wishes of all good Democrats across the length and breadth of the nation. Wallace banners were springing up in the midst of the Alabama delegation. This was impossible, Pauley knew, for Alabama was for Senator John Bankhead and the mere mention of Wallace was enough to start another War Between the States.

It was a moment heavy with portent for the history of the American presidency, but it was a moment in which the tough leaders of the party confronted amateurs. They were not going to put up with nonsense. "I had been greatly impressed by the way Wendell Willkie had stampeded the Republican convention in 1940, largely through demonstrations at the convention hall itself," Pauley remembered, "and I certainly wasn't going to take a chance on Wallace followers wrapping him up as a little present from on high."[31] Within minutes the leaders brought that shouting, cheering, volatile crowd of thirty-five thousand people under control.

The first move was by Pauley, who turned to his convention second-in-command, Neale Roach. "Stop that organ!" said he.

This was not so easy, as the organist did not have a telephone with a bell but with a light. The bell would have gotten his attention; the light, which he could see easily enough, was above one of the manuals, and he could, if he wished, ignore it, which he obviously was doing. "Tell me how?" asked Roach. "He won't answer the phone."

"Get an ax," said Pauley.

Roach told his assistant to get a fire ax and stop the organ any way he could—presumably by cutting its cable.[32]

Meanwhile Kelly informed Hannegan that he, Edward J. Kelly, mayor of Chicago, had the right to declare an overcrowded hall a fire hazard. Hannegan designated Mayor Lawrence, completely reliable, to move adjournment. Eyes glaring, face red, he turned to the permanent chairman, Jackson, a Wallace supporter, a sad, lumpy figure standing in apparent helplessness below the dais. "You get up there right not and I mean now," he shouted, "and recognize Dave Lawrence, or I'll do it for you!"[33]

Jackson, sweating, did as he was told. "This is getting serious," he muttered, barely audible above the din. "People may be injured. We are packed in these aisles until it may become dangerous."

Hannegan had warned Jackson earlier that "he was Hannegan's chairman and, by God, not to forget it!" Hannegan's chairman now announced, "This has been a great day and tomorrow will be another great day." He recognized Lawrence, who at 10:54 P.M. moved a recess until the next morning. Jackson called for ayes and nays, heard shouts on both sides, and ruled the motion carried, with adjournment until 11:30 A.M. One of Hannegan's assistants, now in charge of the organist, thereupon told him to play really loud so as to create a moment of confusion after Jackson adjourned the session. Then to bring home the reality, the party leaders cut off the mikes and got the spotlight operators on the phone, who cut the spots on the platform, putting it in semidarkness.[34]

2

A few years later Mayor Kelly recalled that after the attempted stampede on Thursday night the President of the United States called up the party leaders and said, in so many words, "What the hell's going on there? Are you letting this thing get out of hand?" Kelly told the president that everything was under control. But it was in fact a difficult situation, as Kelly later admitted.[35]

That same Thursday, sometime before the chaotic evening session, reporters met with Senator Truman, and one of them told him he seemed in good humor. "Yes, I am going to be nominated for Vice President," he replied.

"You seem to be pretty certain of it," someone said, egging him on.

"You don't think I'd make a statement of that kind unless I was pretty sure that I knew what I was talking about," the senator answered with a smile.[36]

At that precise moment Truman needed to exude confidence. His situation was by no means clear, even though Roosevelt and the leaders were doing their best to have him chosen as the nominee. The leaders thought they could bring the delegates around, but they could not be sure. They had no idea the Wallace supporters would attempt to stampede the convention that very night, immediately after the president's radio address, using the applause it generated to turn attention to their candidate and hoping that even though the hour was late it would be possible to decide the convention's remaining business. The Wallace people knew the delegates were tired out, surfeited with oratory, ready to go home. The convention's leaders miscalculated this possibility and without the forthrightness they displayed could have lost everything.

Prior to the evening session Hannegan made one move that helped Truman, although it was not totally successful: he released the president's letter saying that Roosevelt would be happy to run on a ticket with either Truman or Douglas:

The White House
Washington

July 19, 1944.

Dear Bob:—

You have written me about Harry Truman and Bill Douglas. I should, of course, be very glad to run with either of them and believe that either one of them would bring real strength to the ticket.

Always sincerely,
/s/ Franklin D. Roosevelt

Honorable Robert E. Hannegan,
Blackstone Hotel,
Chicago, Illinois.

Earlier in the week the chairman had let it be known he had the letter. This was necessary because the president himself told Byrnes about it Tuesday morning, and in his disappointment Byrnes and his partisans were bound to talk about it. The chairman had shown the letter to Truman, probably on Monday night. As he had done with the Wallace letter, he and the other leaders thereafter tantalized doubting delegations and reporters by talking about it. Meanwhile Mrs. Hannegan kept the letter in her pocketbook, and at night she put it under the mattress and slept on it.[37]

When Hannegan released the letter and its text appeared in morning newspapers on Friday, July 21, it naturally excited comment. Some had been generated in the chairman's press conference when he explained the letter's history with a touch of exaggeration, maybe Irish exaggeration. "Some time ago I received requests from Missouri delegates on how President Roosevelt looked upon the possible candidacy of Senator Truman," he said, "and I also was asked about how he felt about the nomination of Justice Douglas." With Roosevelt's consent he was releasing the letter. Reporters at the conference had noticed its date, Wednesday, July 19. The chairman miraculously received it within a single day, with Roosevelt there on his train proceeding toward an undisclosed designation. They knew, also, he had had it several days, for he had been talking about it since Monday. This meant he received it before it was written. "When did you get it?" someone asked.

"It is dated July 19," he replied, perhaps with a grin.

"May I ask why your letter of inquiry to the President was limited to two men when other candidates for the nomination were known to be in the field?" a reporter asked.

"I had on other occasions discussed in general with the President a number of other possible candidates," Hannegan replied. "A number of persons, some of them in Washington, had asked me about Justice Douglas."[38]

To this explanation would be added other confusions, worth setting out in passing. For one, Truman remembered a different handwritten letter that did not mention Douglas, and insisted that Hannegan showed him that letter, not the "Truman or Douglas" letter. As he recalled, it said only, "Bob, it's Truman. FDR." It was "written on a piece of scratch paper about two inches by eight and it had only one name mentioned in it and that was mine."39

How to explain the memory of Roosevelt's successor, who would not have confused the text, especially omission of Douglas's name, in a letter so fraught with meaning for his future? The national chairman's son, William P. Hannegan, has ventured the possibility that his father, showing the letter to Truman in hope of convincing him he was Roosevelt's choice, held his thumb over Douglas's name.

Another confusion about the letter is that the president's private secretary, Grace Tully, asserted in her memoirs that the letter as originally written put Douglas's name first; when Hannegan emerged from Roosevelt's compartment aboard the train in the Chicago yards, he instructed her to juxtapose the names. She gave the letter to her assistant for retyping, and both Grace Tully and Dorothy J. Brady claimed the juxtaposition took place.40

To this it is impossible to respond, other than that memories necessarily differ. It is possible Hannegan gave the Wallace letter to Tully for retyping and she confused the two. Moreover, Justice Douglas wrote a foreword to Tully's book, and it is possible that in his own interest he told Tully what he believed was the original order of names, and she took his explanation. As for Dorothy Brady, hers is no testimony to take lightly; that she corroborated Tully is a disquieting fact in a puzzle that may never be solved.41

Instead of relating confusions it may be more important to consider what the introduction of Douglas's name by the president, presumably in the original handwritten letter given to Hannegan at the end of the leaders' meeting, had to do with events during the convention's final day, Friday. Here it is possible to be unequivocal: it made no difference. For Douglas supporters the principal problem was that as long as Wallace was in the race they had no place to go. Douglas's candidacy appealed to the same individuals who already had lined up with Wallace. Any serious Douglas movement could not begin until Wallace was out. Ickes, an indefatigable Douglas supporter, did his best to discourage the Wallace movement. But as long as Wallace could stay in the race Douglas was out of the race. Douglas may not have committed himself as far on civil rights as Wallace had, or possessed quite the notoriety, one might describe it, for his other liberal views, but he was simply too much like the vice-president.

Douglas also had no judgment about how to advance his candidacy. He should have gotten acquainted with party leaders, but he never bothered, save for a few chance encounters and conversational pleasantries. And the convention assuredly was no time to take himself, as he did, off to the Oregon wilds, on a pack trip to the high Wallowa Mountains, where he was completely inaccessible. Nearly a week after the convention was over, on July 27, he wrote the president: "So it was only yesterday after my return to our summer place that I learned of your letter to Hannegan." He made light of any effort to organize support at Chicago. "Some of the boys were whooping it up for me—much against my will. But I succeeded prior to the Convention in subduing that mild uprising."[42]

Nor was this the total of Douglas's liabilities. Just before the convention Ickes learned from the Washington lobbyist Thomas G. Corcoran that the president's daughter, Anna, had been inquiring about Douglas's drinking habits. Ickes apparently forgot about this inquiry until more than a year later. In November 1945, after Truman was president, Anna and her husband came out to Ickes's country place for a visit, and someone got on the subject of drunken women. She said her father could not stand drunken women—that one weekend at Pa Watson's place in Virginia, Louise Hopkins, the president's assistant's wife, was so drunk that she fell out of her chair. She confirmed that Admiral McIntire said Hopkins himself would stay away from whiskey for long periods and then drink and drink after a doctor told him he was better. But the most interesting part of this discourse had to do with Douglas. Anna was contrite, Ickes recorded, for having thrown her influence to Truman for vice-president; she now thought Truman a little man. She did not think, however, that Douglas would have done any better. She said she had seen Douglas drunk out West on two or three occasions, surrounded by people of a low type. "My conclusion," Ickes wrote, "was that, whereas the President might have designated Bill Douglas for Vice President, if Anna Boettiger had been for him, she threw her weight the other way. The result is that Truman got the chance that, in my opinion, Bill Douglas will probably never get again."[43]

Ickes may have discovered Douglas's fatal defect. Roosevelt liked to think of himself as a daredevil sort of man, a little risky in ventures, and was drawn to the raffish justice. Still, as Anna testified to a friend of Wallace, he was warm in personal relations but coldly calculating in politics, and no daredevil attraction would have persuaded him to choose Douglas. Walker noticed the president's attraction and thought that if somehow the president could have followed his inclinations he would have gone to Douglas, but that in the end he made a careful judgment and included Douglas in his letter only as a sop to Ickes and Mayor Kelly.[44]

The letter endorsing Truman, despite mention of Douglas, was effectively an endorsement of the Missouri senator, and it constituted the first line of attack of the pro-Truman forces. The second line was more complicated, more difficult; it involved soliciting state delegations collectively and individually, talking at meetings and buttonholing delegates in corridors and anterooms, converting them to what the leaders knew—and after release of the letter the delegates knew—was the president's choice.

In the effort to convert delegations, which meant changing the votes of many, many Wallace supporters, McCullough has written that the leaders were up all Thursday night, and that they used every persuasion.[45] But this surely is not what happened. For one thing, after the acceptance speech by the president and the attempt by the Wallace-ites to stampede, the leaders could collapse into their beds. The convention did not reassemble until 11:30, which gave time for leisurely breakfasting, with delegate talk and possible conversions. In the afternoon came vice-presidential nominating speeches, each followed by seconding speeches, oratory that required no thought by anyone, so Chicago Stadium could become a beehive for work with delegations and individual delegates—much as happens during speeches in the national Congress where no one listens and only a few people are on the floor. For another thing, Truman's biographer, in writing that it was impossible to estimate how many ambassadorships and postmasterships were handed out, is probably again off the mark. The embassies belonged to Roosevelt, not the leaders. As for postmasterships, Walker, in his autobiographical writings, said nothing about them. He would have had only a few, for civil service vastly diminished his ability to bring joy to worthy fathers and mothers, widows and orphans. McCullough is thinking of the nineteenth century, the setting of several of his books, when postmasterships held together both political parties, especially the Republican party, impossibly weak in the South, which every four years gave the impression it was a national party by holding postmasters' conventions.

In getting votes for Truman the procedure was not to stay up all night and offer ambassadorships and postmasterships. It was, first, to get a good night's sleep and, second, go around to delegations the next morning and afternoon and spread the word, which was that the president wanted Truman. Hagerty of the *New York Times* learned that Pauley, whom no one ever accused of being a theorist, in addressing the California delegation said, "In my opinion, President Roosevelt is convinced that Truman would cost him less votes than any other candidate."[46] This was the argument.

Truman himself was furiously busy all Thursday night, but not with ambassadorships or postmasterships. He wanted his fellow senator from Missouri, Clark, to nominate him, and could not find Clark anywhere. The son of Champ Clark, the Speaker of the House of Representatives during the Wilson administration who nearly beat out Wilson in the race to be the Democratic nominee in 1912, Bennett Clark was a great Missouri orator, a quick-witted stumper par excellence, better than Senator Kerr. Clark, however, was certainly drunk this night; the only question was where. It was Truman's task to find and program him. He found him at 6:30 A.M., Friday, in a room on the top floor of the Drake. He could not get in, and finally was able to follow a valet with a suit of clothes. When he told him what he needed, Bennett could not talk, just mumbled. The arrangement was to sober him up with a big pot of coffee and get him to work. Truman asked the Missouri state chairman, Sam Wear, to prepare a substitute speech in case Bennett showed up still drunk.[47]

Late in the afternoon the nominating speeches—twelve of them, for Wallace and Truman and Barkley and all the favorite sons— followed by the seconding speeches came to an end. Hannegan's chairman, Jackson, then received his marching orders, which were to start a roll call immediately, for the leaders had arranged to do in the Wallace-ites with several remarkable pieces of shrewdness. For one, by avoiding going into an evening session they controlled their audience, with no chance for a repetition of what happened the night before. For another, instead of asking delegations to vote for Truman on the first ballot, they instructed state leaders either to let Wallace supporters have their way and vote, or give delegations to favorite sons—there were enough of the latter, they made certain, to prevent Wallace from winning on the first ballot. The initial roll call showed Truman with 319½ votes and Wallace in a strong position with 429½, not far from a majority, 589. This made his supporters feel good, but they were unready for the leaders' next maneuver, which Chairman Jackson, on the second roll call and under Hannegan's watchful eye, immediately moved into.

In the way the leaders had arranged things the second roll call had a foregone conclusion, but they kept it from view, so much so that most of the convention delegates did not know what was going on. After the first ballot Ickes rushed up to Walker and kept repeating, "It's going to be an impasse. We've got to do something, Frank. I'll see you after this ballot." Even the chairman, Jackson, "the Honorable Sam Jackson," as Walker described him, was all excited after the first ballot. The Indiana senator thought the lightning might strike himself. "And why shouldn't the lightning strike on the banks of the Wabash?" wrote Walker; he was amused to see Jackson at last in motion, having decided he "wanted in" as a compromise candidate for the vice-presidency. On the rostrum the senator could not be too obvious about his self-inspired boom. He surreptitiously tried to get the attention of Senator Kenneth McKellar of Tennessee, to obtain his support. McKellar was eighty years old and carried his years well, but he was deaf and could not grasp what Jackson feverishly was whispering. "What's that?" he kept repeating. "*What's that?*" Embarrassed, Jackson abandoned his "newly hatched ambitions" and returned to the role of Hannegan's chairman.[48]

Everything then proceeded according to plan. Walker was so sure the convention was under control that after holding Ickes's hand he walked out of the stadium and went back to his hotel.

First on the roll call was Alabama. Pauley had been working on the delegation, which pledged to Bankhead on the first ballot. Delegates said they needed two minutes to persuade the senator who was holding out. "I reached up trying to grab Senator Jackson's leg," Pauley wrote, "but I was too late in getting his attention." Twenty-four Alabama votes went for Bankhead. A solitary delegate on the floor, stationed there for such an occasion, voted the delegation, having not been informed of the problem.[49]

The California delegation proved impossible to vote as a group because of the ten Wallace supporters, including Helen Douglas, all of whom went down with Wallace's ship. To Pauley's disgust, Attorney General Kenny was playing both ends against the middle, "waltzing" the Wallace and Douglas camps while assuring others he was for Truman, but only on the third or fourth ballot. California, like Alabama, proved a disappointment, especially to Pauley, because it was his home state. It gave forty-two votes for Truman, ten for Wallace.[50]

With those exceptions everything went like the clock the second roll call was supposed to be. Governor Herbert R. O'Conor of Maryland agreed to go for Truman if someone would yield or as soon as the state was called. Soon thereafter came the turn of Governor Kerr of Oklahoma. Pauley pointed his finger at him, the signal for Truman, and thought Kerr looked a little pale; he was a favorite son and because of his splendid keynote speech sensed his popularity among the delegates; but he voted the Oklahoma delegation the way he was supposed to. "Under the unit rule," he said in a firm voice, "Oklahoma casts twenty-two votes for Truman." From that point on, the delegations could not get on the bandwagon fast enough.[51]

In a matter of minutes it was a landslide: 1,031 votes for Truman, 105 for Wallace. When Iowa was called the delegates went for Truman, with even Wallace voting for Truman.

— 4 —

"I SHALL CONTINUE. . . ."

After Truman won, the reporter Alistair Cooke, standing below the auditorium at a lunch counter, suddenly heard the voice of the convention chairman say, "Will the next Vice President of the United States come to the rostrum?" He was standing next to a man who had "very shiny glasses, a very pink face, almost an electric blue polka-dot bow tie, and a sky-blue double-breasted suit." The man was holding a paper cup of Coca-Cola and was about to bite into a hot dog. The voice repeated itself, "Will the next Vice President come to the rostrum? Will Senator Truman come?" The man said, "By golly, that's me!" and dashed off.[1]

The candidate made an acceptance speech from a sheet on which he had scribbled a mercifully few words: "Honor. I've never had a job I didn't do with all I have. I shall continue in the new capacity as I have in the U.S. Senate, to help the commander in chief to win the war and save the peace. I have always been a supporter of Franklin D. Roosevelt in domestic and foreign policy and I shall continue to do just that with everything I have as V.P."[2]

Just before the speech, and upon hearing that Truman had won, Helen Douglas promptly fainted. In the general pandemonium fellow Californians helped her off the floor, and Pauley's assistant, Neale Roach, the same who had planned to end the Iowa corn song on Thursday evening by cutting the convention organ's cable with a fire ax, seized Mayor Kelly's car to take her back to her hotel; the driver of the car was one of the mayor's most trusted aides. Mrs. Douglas revived on the way to the Loop and launched into a tirade against Senator Truman, describing him as just another member of the Pendergast machine, a dire reactionary, as typical of boss politics as was Mayor Kelly or Ed Flynn. Every liberal Democrat in the country, she shouted, might as well quit, considering that Truman was in. The driver dropped her at the hotel and hurried back to the stadium to find the convention adjourned and Mayor Kelly fuming, looking for his car. Another man got in with the mayor, and as they went off the driver sought to explain where he had been. He related everything Mrs. Douglas said, and there was a slight silence. The other man happened to be Harry S. Truman.[3]

Helen Douglas would not have agreed, but in long retrospect it does seem that she had just witnessed an extraordinary convention in which a strong leader managed to convey the presidency to another man of equal strength. Despite its flaws the American political system could produce wonderfully competent officeholders. Truman was not the perfect politician, as many people observed during his presidency. He had weaknesses in measuring people, especially domestic politicians. He was much better at choosing individuals to conduct foreign and military affairs, even though he could make mistakes in those areas, as in his choice of Byrnes as secretary of state in 1945, or Louis Johnson as secretary of defense in 1949.[4] He wrote off criticism as politically inspired, which much of it was, but some was for the good of the country, and he failed to understand that. As his nearly two full terms approached their end he became tired out and made mistakes for that reason. Still, he always acted out of ineradicable faith in the virtues of the American people. He knew no pessimism or cynicism; these qualities that warp judgment were foreign to him. He understood he came from the land of opportunity, for opportunity came to him. All in all he displayed a better mix of political traits than his predecessor, Roosevelt. Like Roosevelt he had a real liking for people and yet combined it with a political realism that, unlike Roosevelt's, was not cold-blooded. Unlike Roosevelt he was open, aboveboard, frank, never secretive or manipulative.

A second point about the choice of Truman as Roosevelt's successor has been made by Truman's biographer McCullough, who has written that the boss system, so much maligned, worked well in 1944. He compares it rightly, and critically, with the arrangement of more recent presidential elections whereby candidates are forced to go into state primaries to secure delegates to national conventions, with all that means for homogenization of candidacies. Truman was a product of the boss system in Kansas City, and he was nominated in 1944 by the boss system.[5]

The biographer might have elaborated on perhaps the leading principle of the boss system that Roosevelt violated in 1944: the need to tell the truth. President Roosevelt elevated untruthfulness to a high art. Roosevelt biographers have been tempted to excuse the president's lapses as half-truths necessary to all people in small matters and political leaders in large. The truth is that Roosevelt went well beyond the political pale. The president passed small untruths off as fibs, unworthy of attention; as for honest-to-goodness lies, he denied he made them. All of which is reminiscent of one of Sam Rosenman's favorite stories, about Roosevelt and the Pittsburgh speech in 1932 in which FDR said he would cut the national budget by twenty-five percent. In 1936 the president called in Rosenman and proposed to go back to Pittsburgh and explain everything, telling Rosenman to prepare a nice speech. The judge tried and failed, and went to the president and said he had found the solution. Roosevelt asked what it was. Sam told him to just deny he ever made any speech there.[6]

The bosses did not lie to each other. They were all devout Catholics, going to Mass each Sunday, some of them more than that; years earlier the nuns had taught them not to lie. But quite beyond religion was the fact that politics worked better if a man's word was his bond. Tom Pendergast always acted that way, and Truman many times remarked how thankful he had been to deal on so many occasions with an honest man. Boss Tom, Truman said, seldom gave his word, but never went back on it. Hannegan had been aghast with the president's two-faced statements, remarking the first time, point-blank, that he could not call the president a liar, the second time that "he never hoped he would see his children again if the President did not tell him that." Kelly told Byrnes that sad evening at the convention, Tuesday, July 18, when Byrnes's vice-presidential boom had collapsed, that Roosevelt was the only man he had ever known in politics "who would stay at the top and not keep his word."

After the convention one of Wallace's principal lieutenants, C. B. (Beanie) Baldwin, told the vice-president a lighthearted story in this regard, about a visit to Democratic headquarters in Washington where he encountered Hannegan's right-hand man, Paul A. Porter.

"You had better get over to the White House and straighten yourself out with Anna Boettiger, the President's daughter," said Beanie. "She told me the other day that you are a son-of-a-bitch because of the way you treated Henry Wallace at Chicago." Porter came right back at him: "You go tell Anna Boettiger, 'So's your old man.'"[7]

A third point about the choice of Truman is much worth mentioning, even though it has been remarked several times. This is the reason Roosevelt was so slow in coming around to Truman—so dangerously slow, for he nearly missed getting Truman, getting instead either Byrnes or Wallace, neither of whom he wanted. Here entered the president's modus operandi for dealing with delicate and personal political issues. It came up on the night of the leaders' meeting when Walker mildly demurred over notifying Byrnes that he was being "passed over." Roosevelt brought him up short, saying that this was the way the game was played. A leader used subordinates for tasks that were disagreeable; it was not wise to have the leader dispense disagreeable facts. The Roosevelt administration saw many examples of the president welcoming enemies into the oval office, charming them, giving every evidence of friendship, whereupon they later received unmistakable evidences of where they stood within the administration. The only trouble with this behavior was that it was so glancing, sideways, and subject to misinterpretation—real or pretend—that it could take far longer to be effective than a simple curt dismissal.

The other part of the reason for the president's delay in naming a running mate was his illness, and this leads to a fourth point: in view of his illness it is remarkable that he kept as closely in touch with the political situation as he did. Jonathan Daniels wrote afterward that he thought Roosevelt in 1944 was delaying many decisions that in time's weariness he thought might solve themselves. He was a very weary man, in need of rest. But contrary to so many detractors after his death, his mind remained keenly alert. When Byrnes telephoned him at Hyde Park and he was just getting up after the overnight train trip from Washington, he was quick-witted enough to tell the assistant president that at the leaders' meeting he, FDR, did not make a decision, that the leaders had told him their decision. It was not true, but he was quick enough to say it. The same held for his phone conversation with Byrnes on Tuesday morning, July 18, when he sympathized with Byrnes and then revealed that Hannegan had received a letter endorsing Truman and Douglas. When he spoke to the assembled leaders the next day, together with the designated candidate, and shouted over the phone that Truman could, if he wished, wreck the party in the midst of a war, and slammed down the receiver, it was the act of a combative, lively leader, even as his own life was nearing its end.

A final observation about the choice of Truman for the vice-presidential nomination in 1944. This is whether the man who became thirty-third president of the United States and seemed to gain the office without trying for it was all the time playing a calculated game, an exquisitely sly (one might say) game, to obtain the great prize for himself.

Here one must say that everything, both in logic and action, says that in the spring and early summer of 1944 the Missouri senator was trying to achieve the office he insisted he did not want. He would have been a strange politician if he had not wanted the most powerful office in the world. He knew about Roosevelt's declining health. He knew he was, himself, an attractive candidate. Because of chairmanship of the investigating committee he had become the Upper House's most outstanding senator, as *Time* magazine described him. During his investigations he had been so even-handed that labor leaders as well as industrial magnates admired him. He had made very few enemies. It was his good fortune that he came from a border state and possessed a moderate record on civil rights, this in early 1944, when the South was threatening rebellion against the Roosevelt administration and southerners were willing to make an issue of Wallace's reelection as vice-president. Word was out in Washington that Wallace was no longer the president's favorite. Wallace knew it, but determined to push ahead, short of an absolute "no," which he knew Roosevelt would not give. This was Wallace's only hope for the presidency. Truman knew that he could constitute the necessary conservative opposition to Wallace. Just before the convention, July 9, he wrote his daughter that many people would give anything to be as close to the nomination as he was.[8]

It was necessary to approach the nomination gingerly by denying he was a candidate. Roosevelt disliked ambitious people; Truman of course knew about that, one of the best-known political facts in Washington. Moreover, his wife was against his candidacy.

Jonathan Daniels, an acute observer, wrote, "Truman so operated that neither the supporters of Wallace nor those of Byrnes could fault him. . . . His reluctance was his armor." At the convention, before the balloting, Daniels was nonetheless startled at the "excessive cordiality" Truman showed him as a member of Roosevelt's staff.[9]

Both at the time and later Truman was curiously silent over whether he wanted the presidency, and this makes one think he wanted it. He was so open a man—so accustomed to speak his mind, a "plain speaker," who wrote more letters to his wife (1,268 have survived, and Bess seems to have burned many others) than any other president, who often jotted down dated descriptions, virtual diary entries, of what he was doing or thinking, who wrote memoranda to himself about what special problems were on his mind, who talked to multitudes of people singly and collectively, in the White House and outside—that his silence on this single subject says a great deal.

Nor did he say he did not want it. "I never did hear him say," said his Missouri friend Harry Easley, "that he didn't want the nomination."[10] Easley was the friend to whom, just after the election of November 1944, Truman confessed, while spending a night in the Muehlebach Hotel in Kansas City, that he knew his election meant the presidency.

If he really did not want the nomination he could have done a "General Sherman": not running if nominated and not serving if elected. He did not do that.

He was accustomed to say he never was a candidate for any public office and the office always "caught up" with him. But it is unbelievable. His fellow senator in 1944, Barkley, thought the lament a pose, and when a few years later he was Truman's vice-president he often chaffed him about it. One night at a banquet the president said the usual thing, and Barkley arose and told the audience the statement reminded him of the Republican he had heard about who thought he would get himself a state job when Kentucky elected its first Republican governor in 1895. The hungry Republican got on his mule and rode from Somerset to the state capital, Frankfort, a hundred miles. He stayed around for six months, and finally, all his money gone and no job, saddled Old Nell and started for home. On the outskirts of

Frankfort he met a friend who asked why he was in such a hurry. "Hurry?" exclaimed the jobseeker. "All my life I've heard that the office should seek the man. Well. I've been here six months and haven't seen an office seeking a man yet. If you happen to run across one after I've gone, will you please tell it that I'm a ridin' out of Somerset Pike, and ridin' damned slow!"[11]

It was, then, an effort to get what any politician would have wanted. He did his best, in knowledge that nothing was certain even after Byrnes withdrew and even after Roosevelt endorsed him openly. He could be none too sure of the result until late Friday afternoon, after the first ballot was over, when Jackson was starting the roll call for the second and Walker was going back to the hotel. It was only then that he could breathe a sigh of relief. He could order a Coca-Cola and hot dog and know he would be the next president of the United States.

NOTES

1. Days of Uncertainty

1. Truman saw very clearly what the vice-presidential nomination in 1944 would mean; on July 9, just before the convention in Chicago, he wrote his daughter that "1600 Pennsylvania is a nice address but I'd rather not move in through the back door" (Margaret Truman, ed., *Letters from Father: The Truman Family's Personal Correspondence,* 55). The literature on Roosevelt's illness and death is now large. After the early and altogether unsatisfactory book by Admiral McIntire and George Creel, *White House Physician,* Dr. Bruenn brought out his "Clinical Notes on the Illness and Death of President Franklin D. Roosevelt." See also the remarkable interview by Jan Kenneth Herman, "The President's Cardiologist." Chapter 2 of the present writer's *Ill-Advised: Presidential Health and Public Trust* rests in part on an interview with Dr. Bruenn of February 16, 1992. Other accounts appear in Bert Edward Park, *The Impact of Illness on World Leaders;* Kenneth R. Crispell and Carlos F. Gomez, *Hidden Illness in the White House;* Robert E. Gilbert, *The Mortal Presidency: Illness and Anguish in the White House;* and Jerrold M. Post and Robert S. Robins, *When Illness Strikes the Leader: The Dilemma of the Captive King.*

2. Letter of June 15, 1946, in Robert H. Ferrell, ed., *Dear Bess: The Letters from Harry to Bess Truman, 1910–1959,* 526.

3. Henry A. Wallace diary, Aug. 16, 1944. This sentence was omitted from John M. Blum, ed., *The Price of Vision: The Diary of Henry A. Wallace, 1942–1946,* 380. In great old age Truman said much the same thing to the writer Thomas Fleming: "He was the coldest man I ever met. He didn't give a damn personally for me or you or anyone else in the world as far as I could see" ("Eight Days with Harry Truman," 56). During his last years the former president was "spacy," his thoughts unreliable, but this is an interesting commentary. To Fleming Truman added a remark he often made in earlier years:

"But he was a great President. He brought this country into the twentieth century."

4. Anna Roosevelt Halsted oral history, May 11, 1973, p. 51. Copy in Anna Roosevelt Halsted Papers, box 12. The president's daughter said the same thing to the writer Richard H. Rovere in an interview of August 16, 1958, folder 1, box 15, Richard H. Rovere Papers. Rovere in 1958 had in mind a book on how Truman received the vice-presidential nomination and accumulated a file of material including several interviews. He signed a contract with a publisher, but for some reason he then gave up the project, perhaps because of the death of Senator Joseph R. McCarthy, which offered an opportunity to do a book on the McCarthy era. He published that book the next year. His *Arrivals and Departures: A Journalist's Memoirs* offers no explanation for dropping the proposed book on Truman.

5. Edwin W. Pauley with Richard English, "Why Truman Is President," 4, undated, "The President," box 30, White House central files, confidential files, Truman Library. For the shift to Truman during the first months of 1944 see Brenda L. Heaster, "Who's on Second?" General Watson passed on to the president any letters critical of Wallace, such as the following: "The only reason for the writing of this letter is that this section of the country is bitterly opposed to Wallace for Vice-President. Use that as you will" (Tom Anglin to Watson, Feb. 10, 1944, box 11, Edwin M. Watson Papers). Watson wrote to Anglin, "I showed your letter to the President. Obviously he did not make any comment, but he read it very carefully and thanked me for showing it to him" (Feb. 18). And again: "At an appropriate time I wish you would bring this note to the President's attention. I think it is a mistake to renominate Mr. Henry A. Wallace. There would be no trouble in the south today except for the belief that the President will insist upon Wallace. Many, many democrats who like President Roosevelt, are somehow very, very much against Wallace. I believe it would be a mistake to put him on the ticket. . . . I believe that Wallace's name on the ticket will cost three million votes" (C. J. Harkrader, publisher of the *Bristol* [Va.–Tenn.] *Herald Courier,* to Watson, June 15, 1944, box 8, Watson Papers). Watson wrote on a buckslip, "Respectfully forwarded to the President." Afterward a secretary queried him, "Should this be acknowledged? It is derogatory to the Vice

President and ordinarily would not be answered." The general acknowledged it.

6. For Pauley's activities see the above-mentioned draft article with Richard English, "Why Truman Is President," together with his undated memorandum for Jonathan Daniels in the Daniels Papers. Daniels solicited the account in preparation for his biography of Truman, *The Man of Independence*.

7. Frank C. Walker autobiography, 210. The present writer has brought together this manuscript autobiography from drafts Walker left in his papers, box 123, in the archives of the University of Notre Dame. It is difficult to know how far Byrnes pushed his case with Roosevelt at this time. One has the impression that not much happened, although Byrnes was measuring every comment he heard. His close friend, Walter J. Brown, relates in *James F. Byrnes of South Carolina: A Remembrance* that on June 12 Hannegan and Byrnes spent two hours talking over the political outlook, that Hannegan urged Byrnes to consider the vice-presidential nomination, and that Byrnes on June 17 went to the president's retreat on the Catoctin Mountain ridge in Maryland, Shangri-La, but that Roosevelt did not discuss the vice-presidency. Brown also relates that Hannegan and Roosevelt talked on June 27 concerning Byrnes, and Hannegan immediately came over to Byrnes's office and repeated the conversation. "If you will agree to Justice Byrnes," the national chairman told the president, "we can sail through the convention and the election." "That suits me fine," the president replied. Brown wrote the conversation in his diary or "log," also that "This was the day JFB was tagged for Vice-President." In his book Brown concluded, "Then Roosevelt and Hannegan agreed on Byrnes for Vice-President." But Brown's conclusion does not follow from the conversation—from Roosevelt's remark to Hannegan that Byrnes "suits me fine." Given the president's well-known playfulness in conversation, his tendency to "throw out" remarks, Brown (quoting Byrnes who was quoting Hannegan) made a leap in judgment. Byrnes himself was wary. "Now, partner, let's not get too excited on this Vice-President business," he told Brown. Byrnes did not declare his candidacy until Tuesday, July 11 (for which see below). A list of the invitees to the presidential dinner and discussion that evening, now in the Roosevelt Library, includes Byrnes's name, which someone lined out, evidently that day.

8. Douglas and Frankfurter were frequent White House visitors. The president, for his part, did not hesitate to advise them on the government's court positions. When the administration took a case to the Supreme Court involving the labor leader Harry Bridges, FDR worried about it, and suggested to Attorney General Francis Biddle "that I 'slip a word to Felix or Bill that he would just as leave if the Government got licked'" (Francis Biddle diary, Mar. 16, 1945, courtesy of J. Garry Clifford).

9. Samuel I. Rosenman oral history, 1968–1969, by Jerry N. Hess, 19–22. Another reason may have accounted for the exclusion of Kaiser. According to Secretary of the Interior Harold L. Ickes, "Rosenman was still moaning about Kaiser. I asked him whether he wanted to make anti-Semitism an issue. He said that Kaiser was not a Jew. My answer was that a lot of people thought that he was and many would believe it, with the result that the effect would be the same" (Harold Ickes diary, July 9, 1944). Ickes dictated his diary every few days and the date of an entry is not necessarily the day something happened.

10. The presidency surely has enormous attraction, and Pauley believed Rayburn receptive. Years later the perennial Speaker of the House claimed he was not receptive: "Swears he never wanted Pres. & as for V-P, 'I don't want to be *vice* president of anything'" (Interview of May 21, 1958, folder 1, box 15, Rovere Papers). The interviewer was unconvinced: "Says all aware of FDR's failing. Next VP would be next P. This casts shadow on statements re not wanting VP job."

11. Rayburn interview of May 21, 1958, loc. cit.

12. Cabell Phillips, *The Truman Presidency: The History of a Triumphant Succession,* 37. For Truman's years in the Senate see Eugene F. Schmidtlein, "Truman the Senator"; Roger Edward Willson, "The Truman Committee"; and especially Richard Lawrence Miller, *Truman: The Rise to Power,* 262–380.

13. Robert J. Donovan, *Conflict and Crisis: The Presidency of Harry S. Truman, 1945–1948,* xii.

14. Samuel I. Rosenman oral history, by Jerry N. Hess, 47–48.

15. The president was talking to Byrnes: "Jimmy," he added, "I'm too old to start learning people again" (Memorandum by Arthur M. Schlesinger, Jr., of a conversation with Byrnes, Apr. 17, 1953, folder 1, box 15, Rovere Papers). Truman interview with Jonathan Daniels,

Nov. 12, 1949, p. 69, Daniels Papers; Harry S. Truman, *Memoirs: Year of Decisions,* 56; Truman to Harold Moody, May 21, 1952, folder 6068, postpresidential file, Truman Library; taped interview, Sept. 10, 1959, folder 1, box 2, "Mr. Citizen" file, Truman Library; Jonathan Daniels oral history, 1963, by J. R. Fuchs, 89–90; *New York Times,* July 22, 1944.

16. Allen's book was published in New York in 1950, with a second edition ten years later. It is probable that the author read *The Man of Independence* and took much of his account from it. For the July 11 meeting, his oral history, 1969, by Jerry N. Hess, 4–5, refers readers to his book.

17. Alfred Steinberg, *The Man from Missouri: The Life and Times of Harry S. Truman,* 195; Truman interview with Daniels, Aug. 30, 1949, p. 3, Daniels Papers; *St. Louis Post-Dispatch,* Feb. 26, Mar. 9, 1942, vertical file, Truman Library.

18. Harry H. Vaughan oral history, 1963, by Charles T. Morrissey, 71.

19. The document can be found in "Byrnes, James F.," box 97, president's secretary's file, Roosevelt Library, courtesy of Francis Wyman.

20. Years later Rayburn told an interviewer, "Hannegan begged him to believe that he had not been working for HST," and the Speaker of the House believed him (Interview of May 21, 1958, folder 1, box 15, Rovere Papers).

21. Memorandum of a conversation with Hannegan, May 25, 1946, by Robert E. Sherwood, correspondence, p. 122a, Sherwood Papers, courtesy of Charles V. Reynolds, Jr.

22. David McCullough, *Truman,* 322–23; Edward J. Flynn, *You're the Boss,* 181. Flynn was a very heavy drinker, which also militated against his being an effective champion of Truman. Irma Hannegan remembers seeing Flynn drunk. When President Roosevelt at the very last moment put him on the list of individuals to attend the Yalta Conference in February 1945, White House staff members were incredulous. After the conference the president sent him to Moscow to talk to Foreign Commissar Vyacheslav Molotov about the Soviet Union's entering into some sort of concordat with the Vatican. Ambassador W. Averell Harriman detailed a member of the embassy staff, John F. Melby, to watch Flynn, but the Bronx leader stayed on

the wagon throughout his stay (Melby oral history, 1986, by Robert Accinelli, 87–94).

23. Flynn, *You're the Boss,* 181.

24. That afternoon Walker would talk with Thomas F. O'Connor, editor of the *Scranton Tribune,* also the *Scrantonian,* the latter a combined Sunday newspaper. O'Connor was an ardent Truman supporter, having met the senator in 1943. At that time he had told Truman that he, the senator, could be vice-president, and then president, and volunteered, together with a mutual friend, also present, E. M. Elliott, to push the possibility. "Thereafter in my capacity as an Editor and in my contacts with Mr. Walker which were very frequent and friendly," he pushed Truman whenever possible. That afternoon of July 11, 1944, just before the dinner, O'Connor met with Walker, who turned off his telephones and asked for no interruptions, and went through the list of vice-presidential possibilities. Walker named them off and O'Connor opposed each one, save Truman. Walker told O'Connor he was going to champion Truman (O'Connor to Matthew J. Connelly, Jan. 27, 1950, "Vice-presidential experiences," vertical file, Truman Library).

25. Pauley with English, "Why Truman Is President," 13.

26. Pauley memorandum for Daniels, 7.

27. Walker autobiography, 212.

28. Pauley with English, "Why Truman Is President," 14–15. Pauley's memorandum for Daniels is approximately the same. George E. Allen, *Presidents Who Have Known Me,* 128–29, roughly agrees. Walker's autobiography, 213, has the president saying, "Boys, I guess it's Truman." Samuel I. Rosenman, *Working with Roosevelt,* 445, has the president saying, "It's Truman"; Rosenman of course was not present but talked and corresponded with participants.

29. "I'm sorry, Sam," Pauley said, "but it's not your turn. It's somebody else and it can't be you." Rayburn, he wrote, "took it like the man he is" (Pauley with English, "Why Truman Is President," 17).

30. Ibid., 15.

31. Walker autobiography, 213.

32. Jonathan Daniels, *White House Witness: 1942–1945,* 257.

33. Walker autobiography, 213.

34. Pauley with English, "Why Truman Is President," 2. For Wal-

lace and Roerich see J. Samuel Walker, *Henry A. Wallace and American Foreign Policy,* 54–55. Early's story is in the Eben A. Ayers diary, Apr. 23, 1947, for which see Robert H. Ferrell, ed., *Truman in the White House: The Diary of Eben A. Ayers,* 176–77.

35. Luther Huston, "The Vice President Talks of His New Job," vertical file, Truman Library.

36. Alben W. Barkley, *That Reminds Me,* 196–97.

37. Pauley with English, "Why Truman Is President," 2–2a.

38. "Says Mrs. R put heavy pressure on FDR for retention of HAW and for this very reason—as well as because he was generally incommunicative with family on political matters—clammed up. Discussed vp with no one in family" (Interview with Anna Roosevelt Halsted, Aug. 16, 1958, folder 1, box 15, Rovere Papers). "When I saw the President this morning, he brought up the question of Vice President Wallace. He said that Mrs. Roosevelt is trying to force him to insist on Wallace for Vice President" (Henry M. Morgenthau diary, July 6, 1944, courtesy J. Garry Clifford).

39. Walter J. Brown, *James F. Byrnes of South Carolina,* 184.

40. "Recalls suspicion of father when Wallace went to China. Thought he might take wrong people with him. Had Anna check. Believes he distrusted Wallace's way of going about things" (Interview with Anna Roosevelt Halsted, Aug. 16, 1958).

41. Daniels, *White House Witness,* 231–32.

42. When Daniels reported the president's remarks about Byrnes and Catholicism in *The Man of Independence,* Cardinal Spellman denied he had given Roosevelt any such advice (*White House Witness,* 232).

43. Max Lowenthal diary, Nov. 5, 1948, box C-272, Lowenthal Papers. Murray told this to Lowenthal.

44. Rosenman, *Working with Roosevelt,* 440-41.

45. In absence of the president's wife, Anna and John Boettiger dined with the president and Mrs. Rutherfurd on Friday evening. Earlier, in April, the president's daughter had written her husband, then overseas, concerning her father and mother, "I pray I don't get caught in a crossfire between those two!" (John R. Boettiger, *A Love in Shadow,* 254); John R. Boettiger is the Boettigers' son.

46. Ickes diary, July 9, 1944.

47. Ibid., July 16.

48. Wallace diary, "summary of political maneuvering," undated, *The Price of Vision,* 361; Ickes diary, July 16.

49. Wallace diary, "summary . . . ," undated, *The Price of Vision,* 361–62.

50. "Report from Senator Guffey," 12:45 P.M., July 11, "Wallace, Henry A.," box 170, president's secretary's file, Roosevelt Library.

51. Russell Lord, *The Wallaces of Iowa,* 529; Wallace diary, "summary . . . ," undated, *The Price of Vision,* 362–63.

52. Wallace diary, "summary . . . ," undated, *The Price of Vision,* 364; Edwin A. Harris to Richard H. Rovere, May 30, 1958, folder 1, box 15, Rovere Papers. Harris had received a call from a friend who suggested he go see Charles Marsh, brother-in-law of Wallace's secretary, Harold Young; Marsh owned a string of small newspapers in the South. At that time he was living in a townhouse on Q or R or S Street in Washington Northwest. The friend said Marsh wanted to see Harris; Harris found Marsh attired in purple pajamas, with "a corps of secretaries and aides following him about, and they had to step fast as he kept going from one phone to another, answering and making long-distance calls." In the course of his interview Harris expressed some doubt that Marsh was as close to Wallace as he indicated. "All right," Marsh said, "let's try this. If you leave here this instant and catch a cab and go to Wallace's apartment door at the Wardman Park, Hannegan will be coming out the door with a crestfallen look." Harris did as told, and just as he arrived Hannegan came out the door, flushed and angry. "What in God's name are *you* doing here?" he demanded embarrassedly. Harris and Hannegan were old friends, as Harris had covered Hannegan for years in St. Louis, ever since the national chairman had been a ward heeler. The chairman gave him a ride downtown and related that "he had tried, very hard and very unsuccessfully, to induce Wallace to get out of the running for the vice presidency. (He told Wallace he didn't have a chance.)" Marsh later told Harris that Wallace had virtually insulted Hannegan by saying, "I think a lot of your secretary," and by handing him his hat before he was ready to go.

53. Wallace diary, "summary . . . ," undated, *The Price of Vision,* 366–67.

54. Wallace diary, undated (c. July 31, 1944), ibid., 371.

55. "Democratic National Conventions," box 129, president's secretary's file, Roosevelt Library.

56. Robert L. Messer, *The End of an Alliance: James F. Byrnes, Roosevelt, Truman, and the Origins of the Cold War,* 18, considers Byrnes to have been a Rooseveltian straw man, "a credible counter-candidate to Wallace so unacceptable to his supporters that they would settle for a third, compromise candidate brought in at just the right moment." This is an intriguing interpretation but does not consider the disarray with which the president allowed candidates to go forward—it credits the president with far more farsightedness and decisiveness than surely was the case. In any event there is no proof for the straw-man theory. The only other published account of Byrnes's candidacy is John W. Partin, "Roosevelt, Byrnes, and the 1944 Vice Presidential Nomination." The author had just completed his dissertation, "'Assistant President' for the Home Front: James F. Byrnes and World War II." The article on the Chicago convention and its preliminaries appeared at the precise moment Truman's private papers were being opened at the Independence library.

57. Charles G. Ross diary, June 25, 1948, box 21, Ross Papers; James A. Farley diary, Feb. 9, 1946.

58. Walter J. Brown log, July 11, 1944, folder 74 (2), James F. Byrnes Papers.

59. Brown log, July 12.

60. Walker autobiography, 215; Brown log, July 12; James F. Byrnes, *All in One Lifetime,* 221–22.

61. Memorandum by Arthur M. Schlesinger, Jr., of a conversation with Byrnes, Apr. 17, 1953, folder 1, box 15, Rovere Papers; Byrnes, *All in One Lifetime,* 222; Brown log, July 12 [13], 1944. The log is approximately correct in sequence of events but dates frequently are wrong; Byrnes went through the copy in the Byrnes Papers and corroborated Brown's dates.

62. Crowley's activities are recorded in the Brown log. Crowley does not appear to have left papers. When Byrnes was putting together his autobiography he asked Crowley for a memorandum about the convention and its preliminaries, which Crowley sent. Unfortunately by this time Crowley's memory of what happened was poor. See Crowley to Byrnes, Mar. 20, 1956, enclosing a three-page memorandum, folder 76, Byrnes Papers. Roosevelt's relations with Will-

kie in the summer of 1944 have never been satisfactorily explained, probably because the president held his cards, but also because Willkie died in October. Something certainly was going on. Judge Rosenman in *Working with Roosevelt,* 463–70, relates a trip to New York on July 5, at the direction of the president, to propose that Roosevelt and Willkie collaborate in 1948 in establishing a truly liberal political party, which on the Democratic side would drop off the conservative southerners, on the Republican the isolationists and hard-line businessmen. But matters may have gone further than that. The president of the *Des Moines Register and Tribune,* Gardner Cowles, claimed the presence of Ickes in New York in early July, on a mission to offer the vice-presidency (Steve Neal, *Dark Horse: A Biography of Wendell Willkie,* 313–14). The Ickes diary has nothing about such a mission. Nor do the Willkie papers in the Lilly Library (although the papers have nothing on the Rosenman mission). Drew Pearson attended the Republican convention and returned to Washington via New York, where he saw Willkie on July 5 or thereabouts. He then talked to Ickes about nominating Willkie for the vice-presidency on the Democratic ticket. Ickes was not sure it was a good idea. "I decided that the situation had gone too far already to inject such a new and uncertain element. So I have said nothing about the possibility of Willkie to anyone" (Ickes diary, July 16, 1944). Just before leaving Washington for Hyde Park and San Diego, en route to Hawaii, the president on July 13 wrote Willkie asking to see him upon return. Former senator George W. Norris of Nebraska heard a rumor that Willkie might become the Democratic vice-presidential nominee, and protested to Roosevelt, who aboard his train wrote Norris on July 17 that there had been "feelers" a week or so before but there was no danger of Willkie becoming his running mate. At the Democratic convention Pearson converted the chief of Tammany Hall, Edward Loughlin, to a Willkie candidacy, and Loughlin saw Crowley on Thursday, July 20, whereupon Crowley "poured cold water" on the idea; to be sure, by that time Roosevelt had opted for Truman. Crowley did say he had talked with Roosevelt, who was willing to put Willkie on the ticket if the convention wanted him. Thereafter everything became confused. Word of the Roosevelt letter to Willkie got out, and the day after returning from Hawaii the president in a press conference denied having sent it. Privately he wrote Willkie that for a moment he had forgotten he wrote it. Word of the second letter got out, and Roosevelt admitted he was in correspondence. Willkie was furious over this dissembling but contented himself with a public statement proposing that the two not meet until after the election. For this contretemps see Neal, *Dark Horse,* 313–19, and Ellsworth Barnard, *Wendell Willkie: Fighter for Freedom,* 478–86. Such is about all that has become available on relations between Roosevelt and Willkie in 1944. As years passed it perhaps was possible to exaggerate what happened. In preparation for his book Barnard solicited letters from Willkie's friends and acquaintances, among them an Ohio utility executive, A. C. Blinn, who talked with Willkie shortly before the latter's death. According to Blinn, Willkie said that Governor Gifford Pinchot of Pennsylvania, Rosenman, and Crowley all offered the vice-presidency. Willkie, Blinn wrote to Barnard, was inferring that the late president was a colossal liar (letter of Nov. 28, 1958, "1957–1958," box 1, Ellsworth Barnard Papers).

63. Similar activities of Hopkins are in the Brown log.

64. Walker autobiography, 218–19.

65. Brown log, July 12–13 [14], 1944.

66. Byrnes, *All in One Lifetime,* 223. A transcript of the conversation is in "The Vice Presidency—1944," an account Byrnes wrote in 1955, folder 74 (1), Byrnes Papers. Incidentally this account with some rearrangement of paragraphs forms the chapter in Byrnes's book on the Chicago convention. Byrnes probably handed it to his literary assistant, the historian George Curry of the University of South Carolina, and asked Curry to base the chapter on it—which would account for the chapter's failure to include contemporary shorthand memoranda of what happened at Chicago. In a letter to the author of October 27, 1993, Curry is uncertain how that chapter came together.

67. Brown log, July 13 [14], 1944.

68. Truman interview with Daniels, Nov. 12, 1949, p. 65.

69. Byrnes, *All in One Lifetime,* 226.

70. Truman to Charles G. Ross, Jan. 22, 1950, "Political—Vice Presidential nomination—1944," box 321, president's secretary's files, Truman Library. Judge Rosenman put a somewhat different interpretation on Byrnes's phone call to Truman. He believed Byrnes called because he thought Truman's support would help convince the president that Byrnes was a good liberal Democrat (Rosenman oral

history, by Jerry N. Hess, 22–24). But, surely, Byrnes was smarter than that.

71. Jim Bishop, *FDR's Last Year: April 1944–April 1945,* 101–3, asserts that when the president went up to Hyde Park on this occasion, prior to leaving for Chicago and San Diego, he departed at 10:45 P.M. but changed arrival time at Highland, N.Y., opposite Hyde Park, from 6:00 A.M. to 6:00 P.M., allowing for a long layover in New Jersey near the house of Mrs. Rutherfurd, to which the president was driven. He describes the stopover in detail. But this was an impossibility, for although the train did depart Washington at the time Bishop mentioned, it arrived at Highland at 7:30 A.M., and the president left it for Hyde Park an hour later, spending the day at his house and returning to the train at 6:25 P.M. ("Log of the President's Inspection Trip to the Pacific, July–August 1944," box 68, official file, Roosevelt Library). It was the president's custom to leave the capital for Hyde Park very late in the evening so his accompanying staff could receive two days' per diem.

2. Decision

1. For Hannegan's not working for Truman see above, 9-10.

2. David McCullough, *Truman,* 307.

3. For Kelly's boarding the train with Hannegan, see "Log of the President's Inspection Trip to the Pacific, July–August 1944," box 68, official file, Roosevelt Library. Kelly apparently did not remain in the compartment with the president when the latter talked with Hannegan; the chairman, a few weeks later, asserted that he and the president were by themselves (*New York Times,* Sept. 12). Pauley must have been in the party boarding the train; he so wrote afterward, and one must assume that the keeper of the trip log did not mention him because he did not know who he was.

4. James F. Byrnes, *All in One Lifetime,* 226. There is no source for this comment other than Byrnes's autobiography. During the trip west the president's wife wrote several letters testifying that Byrnes probably would be the candidate and recording her disappointment that her husband would not stick with Wallace, but it is clear he was not telling her much. After Truman's nomination she wrote Lorena Hickok: "I'm sick about the whole business but of course not surprised. I don't know myself what F. thought but I know he thought

Wallace couldn't be nominated & told him so" (July 23, 1944, "Roose-
velt, Eleanor 1944–1945," box 57, Anna Roosevelt Halsted Papers).
See also Joseph P. Lash, *A World of Love: Eleanor Roosevelt and Her
Friends, 1943–1962,* 130–32, and especially Richard S. Kirkendall,
"ER and the Issue of FDR's Successor."

5. "We had a rather heated discussion about the Wallace letter and
the change in the letter that I desired to be made" (Hannegan to
Rosenman, May 21, 1949, "Correspondence re Truman Nomination
[Hannegan & others]," box 18, Samuel I. Rosenman Papers).

6. Byrnes, *All in One Lifetime,* 226.

7. Turner Catledge, July 16, in *New York Times,* July 17.

8. Pauley memorandum for Jonathan Daniels, Daniels Papers.

9. Walter J. Brown log, July 16, folder 74 (2), James F. Byrnes
Papers. Brenda L. Heaster, "James F. Byrnes's Labor Pains in 1944:
The Real Thing or a False Alarm?," seminar paper at the University
of Wisconsin, 1990, sets out Byrnes's background with organized
labor.

10. George E. Allen, *Presidents Who Have Known Me,* 130.

11. Byrnes, *All in One Lifetime,* 227.

12. Turner Catledge, *My Life and The Times,* 148.

13. The story originally appeared in the *New York Times,* July 25,
1944. See also Arthur Krock, *Memoirs: Sixty Years on the Firing
Line,* and Catledge, *My Life and The Times,* 147–48. Catledge obtained the story from Mayor Kelly, but because his friendship with
Kelly was too well known he passed it to Krock. The story caused a
furor, with Republicans claiming the Democratic party was run by
labor leaders, the Democrats denying that the president said "Clear
everything with Sidney." Krock had not written "it," and the slight
misquotation gave Democrats a chance for denial. Hannegan actually went all the way and denied anything near "Clear everything
with Sidney." The fact was that Roosevelt "did not say that. Nor did
he say anything else that could have been tortured to convey that
meaning. That story is absolutely untrue. I don't know who invented
it. I presume that Republican orators will keep repeating this favorite fiction until election day in the forlorn hope that some people will
believe it is true. I want to get the record straight and identify this
one as fabricated out of whole cloth" (*New York Times,* Sept. 12,
1944). Hillman's recent biographer believes the president may never

have said it. "And so it may be that the *New York Times* columnist Arthur Krock, who for years was on the friendliest terms with the Republican business community, deliberately concocted a loaded piece of government apocrypha" (Steven Fraser, *Labor Will Rule: Sidney Hillman and the Rise of American Labor,* 532). (Fraser is none too sure, however: "There was enough truth in the story to make it credible.") But it seems beyond doubt that the president told Hannegan to clear Byrnes's candidacy with Hillman and Murray and probably said, "Clear it with Sidney." Krock and Catledge were both expert reporters and could not have been mistaken about what Kelly told Catledge, save for perhaps a single word. Moreover, the president's suggestion of a clearance appears in substance—not in so many words, but a clearance with Hillman and Murray—twice in the Brown log, for July 16 and 17, Sunday–Monday. It is also in a remarkable memorandum that Byrnes made on Saturday, July 22, immediately on return to Washington from Chicago; Hannegan had told Byrnes that everything was set for the nomination, but the president had told him, Hannegan, that "there is one thing I want you to do, and that is clear with Hillman and Murray" ("Telephone Conversation with F.D.R. on Tuesday, July 18, 1944," July 22, folder 74 (1), Byrnes Papers).

14. Frank Freidel, *Franklin D. Roosevelt: A Rendezvous with Destiny,* 557.

15. Harold Ickes diary, Aug. 11, 1944; Apr. 7, 1945. A search of the Sidney Hillman Papers offered no testimonies, either by Hillman or his correspondents. William P. Hannegan on December 4, 1992, telephoned Hillman's daughter, Philoine Fried, in New York, and inquired about this point; Fried was present at the Chicago convention and acted as her father's secretary. She could not remember what President Roosevelt told her father in the oval office on Thursday, July 13, 1944, or in the next few days, or if indeed her father said anything about a presidential instruction.

16. Boxes 26 and 27 of the Edward J. Flynn Papers in the Roosevelt Library contain dictation and drafts for *You're the Boss.* Flynn dictated accounts on various subjects to his secretary, Grace C. Harrington, and the former New Dealer, Raymond Moley, put them into chapter form. Occasionally Flynn's secretary made memoranda of things Flynn told her in confidence, such as "Notes from memory by

gch on off the record talk by EJF, Oct 22, 1945 as to real facts connected with selection of VP candidate in '44." In rearranged form much of the latter memo passed into the autobiography. How much attention Flynn gave to the composition of his book is impossible to say. One has the uneasy feeling that the claim "I browbeat the committee, I talked, I argued, I swore, and finally I got them to come around" may have been the words of Flynn's secretary and got into the book because they caught Moley's attention. Hannegan, for one, thought Flynn's book in error, although whether on this point or not is impossible to say. On September 17, 1947, he criticized the Flynn book to a reporter for the *Washington Post,* Edward T Folliard. (Folliard to Hannegan, Sept. 18, 1947, "Letters from Famous People, 1943–1949 [1 of 2]," box 1, Robert E. Hannegan Papers).

17. Frank C. Walker autobiography, 220.

18. See Byrnes, *All in One Lifetime,* 217–18.

19. Doris E. Saunders, "The Day Dawson Saved America from a Racist President," stands in opposition to the Brown log, July 16, which relates that Dawson did not oppose Byrnes. According to Saunders, Dawson the week before had seen the president, who told him Byrnes might be the nominee. This was enough to disturb Dawson, a Wallace supporter (could the president have been creating trouble for Byrnes?), who drew up for his friend Mayor Kelly a documented record of Byrnes's anti-black and anti–civil rights speeches and actions. Saunders says Dawson talked to Byrnes for three hours at the Blackstone, date unspecified (but apparently Tuesday), and turned Byrnes down, and a few hours later Byrnes withdrew.

20. Walker autobiography, 221.

21. Brown log, July 17.

22. Ibid.

23. McCullough, *Truman,* 312; Truman interview with Jonathan Daniels, Nov. 12, 1949, p. 66, Daniels Papers; "Telephone Conversation with F.D.R. on Tuesday, July 18, 1944," folder 74 (1), Byrnes Papers.

24. "Telephone Conversation with F.D.R. on Tuesday, July 18, 1944."

25. Of course Hannegan had not written a letter of inquiry. But in releasing his own letter of July 10 the president or someone, probably his press secretary, Early, prefaced it with a letter from Hannegan.

26. Byrnes, *All in One Lifetime,* 255.

27. Brown log, July 18. The same account appears in Byrnes's "Telephone Conversation with F.D.R. on Tuesday, July 18, 1944."

28. "Conversation with A. F. Whitney, the afternoon of Tuesday, July 18, 1944," July 22, folder 74 (1), Byrnes Papers.

29. Brown log, July 18. August 24, back in Washington, Byrnes told Brown his estimate of the president: "Walter, he is a sorry fellow. Because he is a Democrat, I have never told anyone how I feel about him. He crawls around, wiggles in and wiggles out. He is a terrible fellow, no backbone, a jellyfish way of doing business" (Walter J. Brown, *James F. Byrnes of South Carolina: A Remembrance,* 218). September 27 he elaborated: "You know, when a fellow guts himself for you, he is a friend, but when he guts you, deceives and misleads you, he is no friend. I have been doing things for that man for twenty-five years. I will never forgive myself for one thing I did. I left my mother on her death bed to go to South Carolina to get the 1932 convention lined up for Roosevelt. There was strong opposition from Governor James Richards and others. The night of the convention, I was called down to the Governor's office to receive the message that Mother suffered another stroke. When I returned, she did not know me. He has not hesitated to gut every friend he had—the only one left is Harry Hopkins and he is just a slave to him." (Brown, *James F. Byrnes,* 222–23). At a dinner of former Democratic national chairmen with President Truman in 1948, at which were present Flynn, Walker, Barkley, probably Hannegan, and Senator J. Howard McGrath of Rhode Island, then national chairman, the conversation got around to Roosevelt; the White House butler, Alonzo Fields, heard such words as "egotism," "vindictiveness," "hallucinations of grandeur," and "deceit" (Alonzo Fields, *My 21 Years in the White House,* 146–47). Fields was shocked.

30. Ted J. Sanders oral history, 1982, by Niel M. Johnson, 29.

31. Truman to Bess, July 13, in Robert H. Ferrell, ed., *Dear Bess: The Letters from Harry to Bess Truman, 1910–1959,* 505; Mary Ethel Noland oral history, 1965, by J. R. Fuchs, 176.

32. Edward A. Harris, "Soothsayer from Lamar," 1–5, undated, enclosed in Harris to Richard H. Rovere, May 30, 1958, folder 1, box 15, Rovere Papers. Harris earlier had written a brief account of this conversation in which he credited Truman with saying, "Hell, I don't

want to be President" (Edward A. Harris, "Harry S. Truman: 'I Don't Want to Be President,'" 4).

33. Truman interviews with Daniels, Aug. 30, Nov. 12, 1949, pp. 3, 66, Daniels Papers.

34. Truman interview with Daniels, Nov. 12, p. 65.

35. Again, as in the decision of the labor leader to oppose Byrnes, the Hillman Papers have no information.

36. Henry A. Wallace diary, Aug. 8, 1944, *The Price of Vision: The Diary of Henry A. Wallace, 1942–1946,* 374. The Murray Papers in the archives in the Mullen Library of the Catholic University in Washington reveal nothing on this point, nor for that matter on any of Murray's activities at the Chicago convention. For the news conference of July 13 see Wallace diary, undated (c. July 31, 1944), *The Price of Vision,* 368; for the Monday statement, *New York Times,* July 18.

37. Ickes was on very friendly terms with Hillman and had helped get the presidential appointment. "Then I told him that, in my opinion, Wallace would not be renominated and that it behooved him and his organization not to miss the boat. He was anxious not to do so. He said that he had been trying for several days to get an appointment with the President and I volunteered to do what I could to help to bring that about. . . . I told Hillman very frankly that I did not think that Wallace could help the ticket if he were nominated and that in my judgment he would not be nominated. Hillman spoke in a friendly way of Truman. I really like Truman and think that he has done a great job but, after all, he did come out of the Pendergast machine and that would be a ready-made issue for Dewey. Hillman indicated to me that he would be willing to take anyone that the President would suggest. Accordingly, after he had gone, I called both Grace Tully and Rosenman to urge them to get this word to the President before Hillman got in" (Ickes diary, July 16).

38. Fraser, *Labor Will Rule,* 531; Matthew Josephson, *Sidney Hillman: Statesman of American Labor,* 619, 622.

39. Wallace diary, Aug. 8, 1944, *The Price of Vision,* 374.

40. Max Lowenthal diary, July 10, Nov. 5, 1948.

41. Frances Perkins oral history, 1955, by Dean Albertson, vol. 8, p. 660.

42. James A. Hagerty, Chicago, July 18, in *New York Times,* July 19; Wallace diary, undated (c. July 31, 1944), *The Price of Vision,* 368.

43. My learned friend, Francis H. Heller, contends that this particular issue was not as keenly appreciated then as later. In 1941 he spent six months working for a Virginia congressman whose wife was office manager and whose younger brother also worked in the office; up and down the hall things were the same. Professor Heller called my attention to the wisdom of Governor James (Kissing Jim) Folsom, Sr., of Alabama, who when challenged about the appointment of friends and relatives asked whether taxpayers would be more at ease if he hired only people he did *not* know.

44. The early financial problems, including the farm mortgage, are in Robert H. Ferrell, *Harry S. Truman: His Life on the Family Farms,* 87–112. When Bess and Mary Jane went off the payroll in April, 1945, the sergeant-at-arms of the Senate was making $8,000 a year, majority and minority secretaries $6,900, assistant majority and minority secretaries $4,800, and Bess was next. In Truman's office Mildred Dryden, clerk, made $2,520, and Reathel Odum, assistant clerk, $2,340. Messengers and laborers made respectively $1,740 and $1,400. On Truman's Senate office staff the wives of his principal administrative assistants seem to have worked, Irene Messall in 1937–1941 and Margaret Vaughan in 1941–1943. During the vice-presidency of John N. Garner (1933–1941) his wife worked in his office. So did wives or relatives of many other senators and congressmen. For the conversation between Evans and Truman see Tom L. Evans oral history, 1962–1963, by J. R. Fuchs, 317–18, 322, 335–37; for the office press release about Bess Truman's work, "HST-Senator," vertical file, Truman Library; for Truman to Bess, Apr. 30, 1942, Ferrell, ed., *Dear Bess,* 474. Concerning his wife's office work the senator himself explained, "She is my chief adviser. I never write a speech without going over it with her. I have to do that because I have so much to do and I never make any decisions unless she is in on them. She also takes care of my personal mail." Aides in Truman's office said Mrs. Truman worked mainly at home and handled correspondence of a personal sort, knowing which person to address as "Dear Bill" or "Dear Mrs. Jones." For her work at home she received from $24.16 to $36.25 each month in addition to her regular salary (unidentified newspaper, July 27, 1944, release from

Herald Tribune Bureau, vertical file). According to another account, "For all practical purposes, Bess had been working as a member of the staff since 1934. She visited the office regularly and signed letters for him and read and handled routine correspondence. More than a few other senators and congressmen had relatives on the payroll to make ends meet. It was risky because a snide opponent or newspaper critic could make it seem corrupt, although it was perfectly legal and even necessary for men who had to live on their inadequate salaries. The Trumans had not felt secure enough to chance it until Dad's reelection" (Margaret Truman, *Bess W. Truman,* 203). In opposition is the judgment of Richard Lawrence Miller, *Truman: The Rise to Power,* 338: "Truman had enough money to support his mother, his mother-in-law, a large Independence residence with full-time servants, a modest Washington apartment with occasional domestic help, private school tuition for Margaret, and obligatory social entertainments for political colleagues and big shots. He may have had trouble keeping expenses current to income, but that's not the same as being poor. If Truman felt poor, and his private writings show that he did, it was only a relative measurement against the far wealthier people he dealt with every day."

45. Evans oral history, 335; Max Lowenthal interview with Jonathan Daniels, Aug. 31, 1949, p. 11, Daniels Papers.

46. M. Truman, *Bess W. Truman,* 227–28, 233–35.

47. Kathleen McLaughlin, Chicago, July 22, in *New York Times,* July 23; M. Truman, *Bess W. Truman,* 230–31, 233, 258. See also Margaret Truman, *Souvenir: Margaret Truman's Own Story,* 73, wherein the daughter wrote of the vice-presidency at a time when her mother and father were both in good health and must have read her book: "My mother was bitterly opposed to it."

48. Truman interview with Daniels, Nov. 12, 1949, p. 66; Robert H. Ferrell, ed., *The Autobiography of Harry S. Truman,* 90.

49. Conversation with William P. Hannegan, who remembers his father telling this story around the dinner table.

3. Roosevelt and Truman!

1. *New York Times,* July 16.
2. Meyer Berger, Chicago, July 17, in ibid., July 18.
3. Ibid., July 16.

4. Chicago, July 15, in ibid., July 16. In all fairness, one must say, reporters may well have misquoted Mrs. Douglas. They were doing their best to create a rivalry. In her autobiography, *A Full Life,* 196, she quoted herself as saying, "I don't like fencing. I have the greatest respect for Mrs. Luce." On her side Mrs. Luce had said she had no intention of getting "into any hair pulling contest with any woman— regardless of what side of the fence she's on. . . . I am for women making greater . . . strides in politics in both parties" (Ingrid Win- ther Scobie, *Center Stage: Helen Gahagan Douglas, A Life,* 152–53). At the convention reporters asked Mrs. Douglas about nail polish, kissing babies, her height, and her weight.

5. Charles E. Egan, Chicago, July 18, in *New York Times,* July 19.

6. "We believe that racial and religious minorities have the right to live, develop and vote equally with all citizens and share the rights that are guaranteed by our Constitution. Congress should exert its full constitutional powers to protect those rights" (Donald B. Johnson, comp., *National Party Platforms,* vol. 1, *1840–1956,* 404).

7. Chicago, July 17, in *New York Times,* July 18. Secretary Perkins vigorously opposed the amendment and disliked the Woman's Party, which wanted it: "They wish to abolish all protective legislation for women, all differences in the way women are treated and the way men are treated." Interviewer: "I think that's perfectly crazy." Per- kins: "Why, of course it's crazy. . . . Their backs ache more than men's backs ache when they stand up on their two feet all day. It's just the way the Lord made them. It's perfectly obvious. There's no political or moral inequality implied or imputed by the require- ment that 'You shall provide seats in factories where women are employed'" (Frances Perkins oral history, vol. 8, pp. 532–33).

8. Turner Catledge, Chicago, July 19, in *New York Times,* July 20.

9. Chicago, July 19, in ibid., July 20.

10. "Democratic Keynote," ibid., July 20.

11. Frank C. Walker autobiography, 222–23. Walker may have erred in dating Barkley's anger from when the postmaster general told the senator about the telephone call to the president and the senator's desire for Truman's nomination. Walter J. Brown, in *James F. Byrnes of South Carolina,* 207, relying on his log, relates how Barkley came to see Byrnes after the latter withdrew; Byrnes told him the president had written a letter favoring Truman or Douglas,

and Barkley "called Hannegan from our suite and told him to kill his nominating speech."

12. Wilson Wyatt, Sr., *Whistle Stops: Adventures in Public Life,* 39; James A. Farley, *Jim Farley's Story: The Roosevelt Years,* 367; Alben W. Barkley, *That Reminds Me,* 190–91.

13. Barkley, *That Reminds Me,* 190–91; Shalett interviews, 28, Alben W. Barkley Papers.

14. James F. Byrnes, *All in One Lifetime,* 230. "Well, Byrnes phoned me after he came back from Chicago. Byrnes was as angry as he could be at Roosevelt. He didn't say a word against Truman. He still thought Truman was open and aboveboard on everything, and he decided that he had been—he took several minutes, saying, in substance, 'Roosevelt has misled me. I thought I had the assurance, it embarrasses me.' and he added, 'I think I'm going to resign right at once this position.' He was out of humor about it, but I knew what he had in mind, and I said, 'Now listen,' when he got through after he talked to me and told me the whole story, I said, 'Jimmy, don't you do that. If you do that they'll accuse you of being a sorehead.' . . . I had never seen him that way before because he usually was smooth and worked out everything" (Marvin Jones oral history, 1970, by Jerry N. Hess, 119–20).

15. Meyer Berger, Chicago, July 20, in *New York Times,* July 21.

16. Chicago, July 20, in ibid., July 21.

17. For the Byrnes conversation with Hannegan see Walter J. Brown log, July 20, folder 74 (2), James F. Byrnes Papers. The night before, Byrnes had sat in the presidential box, and when Governor Kerr mentioned Roosevelt's name and the demonstration broke out, "I remember how shocked I was when he and Mrs. Byrnes and Ben Cohen [Benjamin V. Cohen, Byrnes's assistant] alone did not stand in the ovation for the President" (Jonathan Daniels, *White House Witness: 1942–1945,* 238–39).

18. For the stampedes see Robert F. Durden, *The Climax of Populism: The Election of 1896* (Lexington: University Press of Kentucky, 1965), Paul W. Glad, *McKinley, Bryan, and the People* (Philadelphia: Lippincott, 1964), Paulo E. Coletta, *William Jennings Bryan* (2 vols., Lincoln: University of Nebraska Press, 1964–1969), Donald R. McCoy, *Calvin Coolidge: The Quiet President* (New York: Macmillan, 1967), and Steve Neal, *Dark Horse: A Biography of Wendell Willkie.*

19. Francis Biddle, *In Brief Authority,* 357.

20. Farley, *Jim Farley's Story,* 361; Warren Moscow, Chicago, July 17, in *New York Times,* July 18.

21. Warren Moscow, Chicago, July 17, in *New York Times,* July 18.

22. Chicago, July 18, in *New York Times,* July 19.

23. James A. Hagerty, Chicago, July 18, in *New York Times,* July 19.

24. Ibid., July 16.

25. Chicago, July 19, in ibid., July 20.

26. Turner Catledge, Chicago, July 18, in ibid., July 19; Walker autobiography, 224–25.

27. Edwin W. Pauley with Richard English, "Why Truman Is President," 20–21, undated, "The President," box 30, White House central files, confidential files, Truman Library.

28. Russell Lord, *The Wallaces of Iowa,* 532–34.

29. The present writer is none too sure how Wallace supporters managed to get into the balcony and onto the floor. The explanation offered in the text seems most likely, but its source is a draft article by Drew Pearson, "Dirt Farmer and Dirt Politician," 5, Pearson Papers, courtesy of William P. Hannegan. The columnist, of course, was notorious for careless assertions. Another explanation of what happened is that Wallace-ites counterfeited tickets. A third appeared years later when Rovere interviewed the national publicity director of the Democratic party, Paul A. Porter. According to Porter, during the convention two Wallace lieutenants came late one night to his room in the Stevens and asked for five hundred tickets. Porter told them they were crazy, and explained that if they wanted entrance they could "buy a door," that is, bribe the doorkeeper, or if necessary buy two doors (interview of May 20, 1958, folder 1, box 15, Richard H. Rovere Papers). But this explanation seems unreasonable, for on Thursday night, July 20, Wallace supporters needed thousands of tickets, not hundreds. Too, if Pearson is to be believed, Mayor Kelly had policemen in charge of the doors, and while Chicago policemen at that time were perhaps susceptible to monetary persuasion, they hardly would have dared defy the mayor. A fourth explanation is equally suspect (and incidentally says something about the gullibility of Vice-President Wallace, who apparently believed it). He obtained it from his lieutenant, C. B. (Beanie) Baldwin: "Baldwin

told me that most of the demonstration on my behalf even on Thursday evening was made by people who had gotten in as a part of the Kelly machine but nevertheless were for me. The CIO boys did have 1500 people they wanted to get in on Friday but they simply could not get tickets although the galleries were practically empty. Beanie says the demonstrations for me were mostly by Kelly people and other Chicagoans of no particular affiliation" (Wallace diary, undated [c. July 31, 1944], *The Price of Vision: The Diary of Henry A. Wallace, 1942–1946,* 370). Several years later Wallace still believed the latter: "It was Ed Kelly who controlled the galleries, but at that time I was popular with the membership of Ed Kelly's machine— that's what it got around to" (Henry A. Wallace oral history, 1951, by Dean Albertson, 3413).

30. Pauley with English, "Why Truman Is President," 20.

31. Ibid., 12.

32. Neale Roach oral history, 1969, by Jerry N. Hess, 24–25.

33. Pauley memorandum for Jonathan Daniels; J. Leonard Reinsch, *Getting Elected: From Radio and Roosevelt to Television and Reagan,* 5–11.

34. Walker autobiography, 226; Chicago, July 20, in *New York Times,* July 21; J. Leonard Reinsch oral history, 1967, by J. R. Fuchs, 28–29; Roach oral history, 25–26. During the attempted stampede Senator Pepper was trying to get to the podium to nominate Wallace, and Roach was one of those who blocked the only entrance to the speaker's platform until after adjournment. At that point he let Pepper through. Years later the senator recalled for David McCullough how he had fought his way through to the podium and how railroad labor leader in charge of the gate had let him through, but at the precise moment Jackson adjourned the convention (David McCullough, *Truman,* 316–17). See also Claude D. Pepper and Hays Gorey, *Pepper: Eyewitness to a Century,* 135–36.

35. Edward J. Kelly, "Secret FD Letter Put Truman In," *Chicago Herald Examiner,* May 15, 1947. Kelly was publishing a series of articles, the first two on the 1944 convention, of which this was the second. The articles were perhaps designed to subtract from an appearance in Chicago Stadium by Henry Wallace, by that time a candidate for the presidency on the Progressive party

ticket. The articles were notably inaccurate, but the Roosevelt comment has the ring of truth.

36. James A. Hagerty, Chicago, July 20, in *New York Times,* July 21.

37. Irma Hannegan to Samuel I. Rosenman, undated, "Correspondence re Truman nomination (Hannegan & others)," box 18, Samuel I. Rosenman Papers.

38. James A. Hagerty, Chicago, July 20, in *New York Times,* July 21.

39. Robert H. Ferrell, ed., *Autobiography of Harry S. Truman,* 89; Truman to Samuel I. Rosenman, Jan. 25, 1950, "Political-Vice Presidential nomination 1944," box 321, president's secretary's files, Truman Library. Years later William P. Hannegan and his wife visited Independence and the Truman Library, and the retired president came over specially to talk to him and wanted very much to know if his mother had the above-mentioned letter—he wanted them to look for it.

40. Grace Tully, *F.D.R.: My Boss,* 276.

41. Truman's later attorney general, Tom L. Clark, recalled that he and Hannegan were close; Hannegan knew that Clark was close to Douglas, and if Douglas's name had been first on a typed note signed by Roosevelt, Clark would have known about it. Clark was convinced this did not happen (Tom L. Clark oral history, 1972, by Jerry N. Hess, 25–26). It was, however, no casual remark in Miss Tully's book, for she said the same thing to Ickes (Harold Ickes diary, Feb. 21, 1948). William P. Hannegan on February 15, 1993, telephoned Dorothy Brady, who resides in the Washington area, and asked about the possible juxtaposition; she is certain it happened. The state Democratic chairman in Missouri at the time, and the state's number-two delegate (next to Truman himself) at Chicago, Sam Wear, told John K. Hulston that he personally knew Hannegan switched Truman's name ahead of Douglas's at Chicago. Wear was a close family friend, and his son was Hulston's law-school classmate (Hulston to the author, Sept. 9, 1993).

All in all, one must conclude, the entire issue of Roosevelt's handwritten note and subsequently typed letter to Hannegan is downright perplexing. As for the possible juxtaposition, Hannegan read Tully's book and was "very disappointed" by her story (Irma Hannegan to Frank Walker, Feb. 11, 1950, box 6, Robert E. Hannegan

Papers). As for the possibility that Hannegan possessed a handwritten note from the president that mentioned only Truman, Frank Walker thought that this might indeed have been the case (Walker to Irma Hannegan, Mar. 5, 1951, "Letters from Famous People, Book 1, 1943–1966," box 1, Hannegan Papers). He wrote to ask if Irma Hannegan had any tiny notes around, for one of them might be the chit that Roosevelt gave her husband on Tuesday night, July 11, and it could have mentioned only Truman's name. The next day, Walker believed, Hannegan returned to the White House, received a second handwritten note, and had that note typed. "In other words, it is suggested that on the night before the President scribbled off an even shorter note on a little piece of paper. Then the next morning when Bob was there, the President wrote another slightly longer note and it was this version which was promptly typed and signed 'Franklin D. Roosevelt.'" It does not seem possible that after the national chairman obtained a chit on Tuesday evening he failed to look at it, and if he had seen Douglas's name he surely would have remarked the fact to Walker.

42. Douglas to Roosevelt, July 27, 1944, "Democratic National Conventions," box 129, president's secretary's file, Roosevelt Library.

43. Ickes diary, July 16, 1944; Nov. 14, 1945.

44. Walker autobiography, 215. Douglas's position in regard to the nomination certainly was marginal, but it worried shrewd observers such as Max Lowenthal, and a memorandum of June 28, 1944, in Lowenthal's Papers, box C-27-2, offers an interesting explanation of how Douglas might have been pushed forward. Lowenthal heartily disliked Corcoran, considered Douglas an ambitious hypocrite, and believed the two were in league. The memo carefully described Roosevelt as "the skipper" and Corcoran as "the manager," and considered the possibility that Corcoran, though out of favor with the White House, might be able to advance Douglas by planting in the president's mind, through intermediaries, that there were three canidates—Secretary of Commerce Jesse Jones, Wallace, and the manager's man. The idea was that the manager then would knock off the first two. Lowenthal believed the president wanted someone for vice-president who could take his place in 1948, and that presented a problem with Truman, whom Roosevelt did not consider equipped for the presidency. The way to thwart the manager was to

urge Truman or someone else but relate to the skipper that it was unnecessary to show aptitude for the presidency because it still would be possible, over the next four years, to find someone else and build him up by putting him in the cabinet or some other position of prominence. Interestingly this short memo bears on its first page the initials *MB,* probably its addressee, Maxwell Brandwen. In an undated memorandum of 1948 bearing the title of "Thomas G. Corcoran's Relation to William O. Douglas," in box 2 of the Lowenthal Papers, the author went into more detail. Corcoran's management of the Douglas movement might have been at fault on one crucial occasion, he believed, in 1943 when Roosevelt asked Douglas to become head of a war agency. Douglas said he would have to consult the chief justice, Harlan F. Stone, and instead consulted Corcoran. The latter apparently advised that Douglas might not have to resign from the court, but if he did so he ought to get something worthwhile in return from the president, such as assurance of the vice-presidency. Douglas went to Oregon, and after a long wait FDR telephoned to say that after all, with the war going on, if Douglas was to do any war work he had better get busy and accept. Douglas said he was coming east soon and would talk the problem over. Roosevelt later told friends that throughout the affair Douglas was angling for the vice-presidency and that he, FDR, was not going to pay that price. Whatever the truth of this matter, so Lowenthal thought in 1948, Corcoran in 1944 nonetheless set up his usual three-man group of candidates, easily knocked out Jones, who Roosevelt believed had staged the Texas revolt to get himself the vice-presidential nomination, and then spent too much time knocking out Wallace. He sent various people to Capitol Hill to "do a job on" Wallace. Through them he painted Wallace as "not merely erratic, but actually insane." He got Secretary of the Navy James V. Forrestal to spread the word in private talks with congressional leaders, and indicated to Forrestal that he himself might be vice-president, which would have been all right if he, Corcoran, could not get Douglas. Meanwhile the manager's friends urged upon the skipper that he should not name only one person, for that would look too much like dictation to the convention. Douglas credited Corcoran with arranging Roosevelt's letter, a "ten strike." But Truman was not far enough in front, for a sufficient period, to enable Corcoran to "bump

him off too." There were too many names up until the very end.
"Besides, D had not yet been built up sufficiently." All this caused
Roosevelt embarrassment. "Jimmy Byrnes phoning FDR from Chi-
cago, asked what D had that Jimmy didn't. FDR laughed, and said:
Bill D can play a good game of poker, and he has a fund of good dirty
stories."

45. McCullough, *Truman,* 318.

46. Chicago, July 20, in *New York Times,* July 21.

47. Truman interview with Jonathan Daniels, Nov. 12, 1949, p. 66,
Daniels Papers; John K. Hulston to author, Aug. 16, 1983.

48. Walker autobiography, 223, 226; Pauley with English, "Why
Truman Is President," 23–24. In a telegram to Roosevelt on Friday
morning, just before the balloting, Ickes characteristically ascribed
the convention's management to "city bosses." "You made a great
speech last night to a crowd that packed and overflowed the stadium. But the city bosses issue is growing to a degree that I did not
anticipate when I telegraphed you two days ago [for this telegram,
ending 'What I am witnessing here is in violation of my political
judgment and is creating a grave political hazard,' see Ickes diary,
July 22]. Unfortunately Hannegan for several days circulated the
report that he had a letter from you in which you had expressed
preference for Truman as a candidate for Vice President. He refused
to show the letter until yesterday after the demand had become so
insistent that his hand was in effect forced. Then the letter appeared
not only to be agreeable as to Truman for the Vice Presidency but
equally to Douglas. Moreover the latter was dated the nineteenth
which was after the date when the rumor was first put into circula-
tion. The whole thing has created a bad incident and delegates in
private conversations last night were demanding that Hannegan
resign. Even the *Chicago Sun* has raised the 'city bosses' issue. The
demonstration for Wallace last night at the conclusion of your speech
was impressive, so much so that the management decided to recess
instead of going forward with the plan to nominate if possible last
night. The issue of the city bosses in the event of Truman's nomination in my judgment will cut deeply into the election and may very
well mean the return of an opposition Congress. Feeling four years
ago and you know what that was is not nearly so high nor so bitter as
it is today. J. David Stern has just come in to say that he knows of his

own knowledge that Truman is a Buchmanite and has been one of the active speakers for that movement. This movement is also known as moral appeasement and in England where it originated it is out and out Fascism." The president's press secretary, Early, sent the following telegram to the president in San Diego: "Have received another long telegram from Ickes. He stresses again 'the issue of the city bosses' at the Convention and criticizes Hannegan for not sooner releasing letter regarding Vice Presidential candidates. Am giving the telegram to Harry Hopkins. However, will send you full text if you want it" ("Trip-Pacific-Hawaii-Aleutians-July-August 1944," box 37, Stephen T. Early Papers).

49. Pauley with English, "Why Truman Is President," 15–16.

50. Ibid.

51. Ibid., 24.

4. "I Shall Continue. . . ."

1. Transcript of a program over the British Broadcasting Corporation, May 5, 1984, p. 2, courtesy of Anthony Moncrieff and John Major. Alas for one small portion of Cooke's account: photographs of Friday, July 21, show his subject without a bow tie.

2. Miscellaneous historical documents, box 1, Truman Library. Senator Truman's speech before the convention was slightly different: "You don't know how very much I appreciate the very great honor which has come to the State of Missouri," he said in a halting, shy manner. "It is also a great responsibility which I am perfectly willing to assume. Nine years and five months ago I came to the Senate. I expect to continue the efforts I have made there to help shorten the war and to win the peace under the great leader, Franklin D. Roosevelt. I don't know what else I can say, except that I accept this great honor with all humility. I thank you" (Turner Catledge, Chicago, July 21, in *New York Times,* July 22).

3. Edwin W. Pauley with Richard English, "Why Truman Is President," 25–26, undated, "The President," box 30, White House central files, confidential files, Truman Library.

4. Actually he made these selections for reasons of domestic politics—Byrnes because of shoddy treatment by Roosevelt during the Chicago convention, Johnson for being treasurer of the Democratic national committee during the 1948 election.

5. The president and Hannegan (and all the Democratic leaders) carefully preserved the fiction that the national convention was not boss-ridden. Roosevelt wired Hannegan on July 21, 1944: "You are to be heartily congratulated on your first conduct of a Democratic convention which certainly deserved the word 'democratic.' All good luck" ("Democratic national conventions," in box 129, president's secretary's file, Roosevelt Library).

6. Eben A. Ayers diary, Oct. 19, 1945, Robert H. Ferrell, ed., *Truman in the White House: The Diary of Eben A. Ayers,* 91–92.

7. Wallace diary, Aug. 12, 1944, *The Price of Vision: The Diary of Henry A. Wallace, 1942–1946,* 376–77.

8. Margaret Truman, ed., *Letters from Father: The Truman Family's Personal Correspondence,* 55. As mentioned above (Chapter 1, note 1), the letter admitted that the vice-presidency meant the presidency. Margaret Truman's *Bess W. Truman,* 225, relates that it also was intended for her mother, though addressed to Margaret; it was a way her father could point out to her mother, who hated the possibility of the presidency, that things were getting close.

9. Jonathan Daniels, *White House Witness,* 239–40.

10. Harry Easley oral history, 1967, by J. R. Fuchs, 103, Truman Library.

11. Alben W. Barkley, *That Reminds Me,* 195–96.

BIBLIOGRAPHY

Manuscripts

Barkley, Alben W. Papers. University of Kentucky Library, Lexington.

Barnard, Ellsworth. Papers. Lilly Library, Indiana University, Bloomington.

Byrnes, James F. Papers. Clemson University Library, Clemson, South Carolina.

Daniels, Jonathan. Papers. Harry S. Truman Library, Independence, Missouri.

Early, Stephen T. Papers. Franklin D. Roosevelt Library, Hyde Park, New York.

Farley, James A. Diary. Manuscript division, Library of Congress, Washington, D.C.

Flynn, Edward J. Papers. Franklin D. Roosevelt Library.

Halsted, Anna Roosevelt. Papers. Franklin D. Roosevelt Library.

Hannegan, Robert E. Papers. Harry S. Truman Library.

Hillman, Sidney. Papers. Labor-Management Documentation Center, Martin P. Catherwood Library, Cornell University, Ithaca, New York.

Ickes, Harold. Diary. Manuscript division, Library of Congress.

Lowenthal, Max. Papers and Diary. Archives of the University of Minnesota, Minneapolis.

Murray, Philip. Papers. Mullen Library, Catholic University, Washington, D.C.

Roosevelt, Franklin D. Papers. Franklin D. Roosevelt Library.

Rosenman, Samuel I. Papers, Franklin D. Roosevelt Library.

Ross, Charles G. Papers and Diary. Harry S. Truman Library.

Rovere, Richard H. Papers. State Historical Society of Wisconsin, Madison.

Truman, Harry S. Papers. Harry S. Truman Library.

Walker, Frank C. Papers. Archives of the University of Notre Dame, Hesburgh Library, South Bend, Indiana.

Wallace, Henry, A. Papers and Diary. Microfilm, University of Iowa Library, Iowa City.
Watson, Edwin M. Papers. University of Virginia Library, Charlottesville.
Willkie, Wendell. Papers. Lilly Library.

Oral Histories

Allen, George E., by Jerry N. Hess. Harry S. Truman Library.
Clark, Tom L., by Jerry N. Hess. Harry S. Truman Library.
Daniels, Jonathan, by J. R. Fuchs. Harry S. Truman Library.
Easley, Harry, by J. R. Fuchs. Harry S. Truman Library.
Evans, Tom L., by J. R. Fuchs. Harry S. Truman Library.
Halsted, Anna Roosevelt, by James E. Sargent. Oral History Collection, Oral History Research Office, Butler Library, Columbia University, New York, N.Y.
Jones, Marvin, by Jerry N. Hess. Harry S. Truman Library.
Melby, John F., by Robert Accinelli. Harry S. Truman Library.
Noland, Mary Ethel, by J. R. Fuchs. Harry S. Truman Library.
Perkins, Frances, by Dean Albertson. Oral History Collection, Oral History Research Office, Butler Library.
Reinsch, J. Leonard, by J. R. Fuchs. Harry S. Truman Library.
Roach, Neale, by Jerry N. Hess. Harry S. Truman Library.
Rosenman, Samuel I., by Joseph Wall. Oral History Collection, Oral History Research Office, Butler Library.
————, by Jerry N. Hess. Harry S. Truman Library.
Sanders, Ted J., by Niel M. Johnson. Harry S. Truman Library.
Vaughan, Harry H., by Charles T. Morrissey. Harry S. Truman Library.
Wallace, Henry A., by Dean Albertson. Oral History Collection, Oral History Research Office, Butler Library.

Books, Articles, and Dissertations

Allen, George E. *Presidents Who Have Known Me*. New York: Simon and Schuster, 1950.
Barkley, Alben W. *That Reminds Me*. Garden City, N.Y.: Doubleday, 1954.
Barnard, Ellsworth. *Wendell Willkie: Fighter for Freedom*. Marquette: Northern Michigan University Press, 1966.

Biddle, Francis. *In Brief Authority*. Garden City, N.Y.: Doubleday, 1962.

Biles, Roger. *Big City Boss in Depression and War: Mayor Edward J. Kelly of Chicago*. DeKalb: Northern Illinois University Press, 1984.

Bishop, Jim. *FDR's Last Year: April 1944–April 1945*. New York: Morrow, 1974.

Blum, John M., ed. *The Price of Vision: The Diary of Henry A. Wallace, 1942–1946*. Boston: Houghton Mifflin, 1973.

Boettiger, John R. *A Love in Shadow*. New York: Norton, 1978.

Brown, Walter J. *James F. Byrnes of South Carolina: A Remembrance*. Macon, Ga.: Mercer University Press, 1992.

Bruenn, Howard G. "Clinical Notes on the Illness and Death of President Franklin D. Roosevelt." *Annals of Internal Medicine* 72 (1970): 579–591.

Byrnes, James F. *All in One Lifetime*. New York: Harper, 1958.

Catledge, Turner. *My Life and The Times*. New York: Harper and Row, 1971.

Crispell, Kenneth R. and Carlos F. Gomez, *Hidden Illness in the White House*. Durham, N.C.: Duke University Press, 1988.

Daniels, Jonathan. *The Man of Independence*. Philadelphia: Lippincott, 1950.

———. *White House Witness: 1942–1945*. Garden City, N.Y.: Doubleday, 1975.

Donovan, Robert J. *Conflict and Crisis: The Presidency of Harry S. Truman, 1945–1948*. New York: Norton, 1977.

Douglas, Helen. *A Full Life*. Garden City, N.Y.: Doubleday, 1982.

Farley, James A. *Jim Farley's Story: The Roosevelt Years*. New York: Whittlesey House, 1948.

Ferrell, Robert H. *Harry S. Truman: His Life on the Family Farms*. Worland, Wyo.: High Plains Publishing Co., 1991.

———. *Ill-Advised: Presidential Health and Public Trust*. Columbia: University of Missouri Press, 1992.

———, ed. *The Autobiography of Harry S. Truman*. Boulder: Colorado Associated University Press, 1980.

———, ed. *Dear Bess: The Letters from Harry to Bess Truman, 1910–1959*. New York: Norton, 1983.

———, ed. *Truman in the White House: The Diary of Eben A. Ayers*. Columbia: University of Missouri Press, 1991.

Fields, Alonzo. *My 21 Years in the White House.* New York: Coward-McCann, 1960.

Fleming, Thomas. "Eight Days with Harry Truman." *American Heritage* 43 (July–Aug. 1992): 54–59.

Flynn, Edward J. *You're the Boss.* New York: Viking, 1947.

Foster, James C. *The Union Politic: The CIO Political Action Committee.* Columbia: University of Missouri Press, 1975.

Fraser, Steven. *Labor Will Rule: Sidney Hillman and the Rise of American Labor.* New York: Free Press, 1991.

Freidel, Frank. *Franklin D. Roosevelt: A Rendezvous with Destiny.* Boston: Little, Brown, 1990.

Gilbert, Robert E. *The Mortal Presidency: Illness and Anguish in the White House.* New York: Basic Books, 1992.

Harris, Edward A. "Harry S. Truman: 'I Don't Want to Be President.'" In *Public Men: In and Out of Office*, edited by J. T. Salter, 3–21. Chapel Hill: University of North Carolina Press, 1946.

Heaster, Brenda L. "Who's on Second?" *Missouri Historical Review* 80.2 (Jan. 1986): 156–75.

Herman, Jan Kenneth. "The President's Cardiologist." *Navy Medicine* 81.2 (Mar.–Apr. 1990): 6–13.

Huston, Luther. "The Vice President Talks of His New Job." *New York Times Magazine,* Jan. 21, 1945.

Johnson, Donald B., comp. *National Party Platforms.* Vol. 1, *1840–1956.* Urbana: University of Illinois Press, 1978.

Josephson, Matthew. *Sidney Hillman: Statesman of American Labor.* Garden City, N.Y.: Doubleday, 1952.

Kirkendall, Richard S. "ER and the Issue of FDR's Successor." In *Without Precedent: The Life and Career of Eleanor Roosevelt,* edited by Joan Hoff Wilson and Marjorie Lightman, 176–97. Bloomington: Indiana University Press, 1984.

Krock, Arthur. *Memoirs: Sixty Years on the Firing Line.* New York: Funk and Wagnalls, 1968.

Lash, Joseph P. *A World of Love: Eleanor Roosevelt and Her Friends, 1943–1962.* Garden City, N.Y.: Doubleday, 1984.

Lord, Russell. *The Wallaces of Iowa.* Boston: Houghton Mifflin, 1947.

McCullough, David. "I Hardly Know Truman." *American Heritage* 43.4 (July–Aug. 1992): 47–64.

———. *Truman.* New York: Simon and Schuster, 1992.

McGuire, Jack B. "Andrew Higgins Plays Presidential Politics." *Louisiana History* 15 (1974): 273–84.

McIntire, Ross T., and George Creel. *White House Physician*. New York: G. P. Putnam's, 1946.

Messer, Robert L. *The End of an Alliance: James F. Byrnes, Roosevelt, Truman, and the Origins of the Cold War.* Chapel Hill: University of North Carolina Press, 1982.

Miller, Richard Lawrence. *Truman: The Rise to Power.* New York: McGraw-Hill, 1986.

Neal, Steve. *Dark Horse: A Biography of Wendell Willkie.* Garden City, N.Y.: Doubleday, 1984.

Park, Bert Edward. *The Impact of Illness on World Leaders.* Philadelphia: University of Pennsylvania Press, 1986.

Partin, John W. "'Assistant President' for the Home Front: James F. Byrnes and World War II." Ph.D. diss., University of Florida, 1977.
———. "Roosevelt, Byrnes, and the 1944 Vice Presidential Nomination." *Historian* 42 (1979–1980): 85–100.

Pepper, Claude D., and Hays Gorey. *Pepper: Eyewitness to a Century.* New York: Harcourt Brace Jovanovich, 1987.

Phillips, Cabell. *The Truman Presidency: The History of a Triumphant Succession.* New York: Macmillan, 1966.

Post, Jerrold M., and Robert S. Robins. *When Illness Strikes the Leader: The Dilemma of the Captive King.* New Haven: Yale University Press, 1993.

Reinsch, J. Leonard. *Getting Elected: From Radio and Roosevelt to Television and Reagan.* New York: Hippocrene Books, 1988.

Rosenman, Samuel I. *Working with Roosevelt.* New York: Harper, 1952.

Rovere, Richard H. *Arrivals and Departures: A Journalist's Memoirs.* New York: Macmillan, 1976.

Saunders, Doris E. "The Day Dawson Saved America from a Racist President." *Ebony,* July 1972, 42–50.

Schmidtlein, Eugene F. "Truman the Senator." Ph.D. diss. University of Missouri, 1962.

Scobie, Ingrid Winther. *Center Stage: Helen Gahagan Douglas, A Life.* New York: Oxford University Press, 1992.

Sirevag, Torbjorn. *The Eclipse of the New Deal: And the Fall of Vice President Wallace, 1944.* New York: Garland, 1985.

Steinberg, Alfred. *The Man from Missouri: The Life and Times of Harry S. Truman.* New York: Putnam, 1962.

Truman, Harry S. *Memoirs: Year of Decisions.* Garden City, N.Y.: Doubleday, 1955.

Truman, Margaret. *Bess W. Truman.* New York: Macmillan, 1986.

———. *Harry S. Truman.* New York: Morrow, 1973.

———. *Souvenir: Margaret Truman's Own Story.* New York: McGraw-Hill, 1956.

———, ed. *Letters from Father: The Truman Family's Personal Correspondence.* New York: Arbor House, 1981.

Tully, Grace. *F.D.R.: My Boss.* New York: Scribner's, 1949.

Willson, Roger Edward. "The Truman Committee." Ph.D. diss., Harvard University, 1966.

Wyatt, Wilson, Sr., *Whistle Stops: Adventures in Public Life.* Lexington: University Press of Kentucky, 1985.

INDEX